Discipled by Grace

And other Sermons that Matter

Jack Davidson

Parson's Porch Books

www.parsonsporchbooks.com

Discipled by Grace and other Sermons that Matter
ISBN: Softcover 978-1-949888-39-3
Copyright © 2019 by Jack Davidson

All rights reserved. No part of this book may be reproduced or transmitted in any form or by any means, electronic or mechanical, including photocopying, recording, or by any information storage and retrieval system, without permission in writing from the publisher.

Discipled by Grace

Contents

Sermons Matter 7
The Holy One 8
   Luke 1:35
The Debt of Jesus's Name 13
   Luke 2:21; Matthew 1:21
His Father's House 18
   Luke 2:49
The Christmas Bell 23
   Luke 2:13-14
A Savior for the Stress of Our Sin 26
   Mark 1:32-45
The Mighty Power of Forgiveness 32
   Mark 2:1-12
Discipled By Grace 46
   Mark 2:18-22
The Angry Lord of the Sabbath 53
   Mark 3:1-6
Warning to the World 60
   Mark 3:20-35
The Repentance We Need 66
   Mark 6:1-2,7,12,20
The Leader We Need 72
   Mark 6:30-44

The Heart We Need 78
    Mark 6:45-57, 7:1-30
The Understanding We Need 85
    Mark 8:1-30
The Hosanna Moment 92
    Mark 11:1-10
One Messenger Left to Send 100
    Mark 12:1-12
The Greatest Commandment Ever Told 108
    Mark 12:28-34
The Greatest Commandment Ever Told (2) 114
    Mark 12:28-34
The Victory He Secured 120
    Mark 16:1-20
Hannah's Treasure 126
    1 Samuel 1-2:1

Sermons Matter

Parson's Porch Books is delighted to present to you this series called Sermons Matter.

We believe that many of the best writers are pastors who take the role of preacher seriously. Week in, and week out, they exegete scripture, research material, write and deliver sermons in the context of the life of their particular congregation in their given community.

We further believe that sermons are extensions of Holy Scripture which need to be published beyond the manuscripts which are written for delivery each Sunday. Books serve as a vehicle for the sermon to continue to proclaim the Good News of the Morning to a broader audience.

We celebrate the wonderful occasion of the preaching event in Christian worship when the Pastor speaks, the People listen, and the Work of the Church proceeds.

Take, Read, and Heed.

David Russell Tullock, M.Div., D.Min.
Publisher
Parson's Porch Books

The Holy One

Luke 1:35

> The Holy Spirit will come upon you, and the power of the Most High will overshadow you. So the Holy One to be born will be called the Son of God.   Luke 1:35

Jesus Christ, the Son of God is described as "the Holy One" by the angel, Gabriel. When you photograph someone, you frame their face, the most beautiful part. If the infinite and eternal God could be drawn to life, out of all of His attributes or qualities, holiness would be His face. The Psalmist writes, "Worship the LORD in the splendor of His holiness" (Ps. 96:9, 29:2 c.f. 2 Chr. 20:21, Ps. 27:4). When God speaks of Himself or us, what is emphasized? "Be holy, because I am holy" (1Peter 1:13-16).

We once had such moral beauty but lost it. Genesis 5:1-3 tells us that God created Adam and Eve "in His own likeness" which refers to God's image, especially His holiness. But after the temptation and fall into sin, when Eve gives birth to Seth, the Bible says Adam had a son in *his* own likeness (Gen. 5:3). From the likeness of God, the human race regressed to the likeness of Adam's fallen humanity. In God's eyes, sin has ruined our beauty. It has shot us all in the face at point blank range. We have survived but we're dreadful in His sight. We're like someone whose visage has been ruined by a bullet or a wild animal or some horrible accident. We have been ruined by sin and are cut off from our Creator. We're morally ugly. We've said or done ugly things. Impurities of every kind plague us from within. We have broken or break God's commandments in thought, word, and deed. Job 25:4 states our problem with a question, "How can one born of a woman be pure?"

How can our holiness - a "face" such as ours - be restored? Someone whose actual face has been marred must wait for the death of a donor, a person who gives permission for their own face to be surgically removed at their death and transplanted to a waiting recipient. In a way, our only hope is for such a donor, one with true holiness. The Bible teaches that when we believe in Jesus as the Son of God, we are granted Jesus Christ's own holiness. We know this because the name given in the Bible to everyone who believes in Jesus is "saint" or "holy one." God sets us apart as His own "sanctified in Christ Jesus" and we are "called to be holy" (1Cor.1:2, c.f. Eph. 5:25-27, 1 Peter 1:16). How can this be? As the Holy One, His death on the cross was a sacrifical death for our sins. The book of Leviticus in the Old Testament teaches that this kind of sacrifice is an "atonement" literally, a "covering." All of God's requirements and conditions are met by Him. We are people whose moral visage was disfigured by sin, but the great Donor of heaven, born at Bethlehem, grew up and died. He willed His own face to cover over my own multilated mess. From a moral perspective, by faith in Him, I can look human again. Faith in Him does not actually make us holy or perfect, but "in Christ Jesus" we are now covered, and our relationship to God is restored.

We have not kept God's holy requirements nor the many lesser standards to which we might subscribe. We try to live right, eat right, parent right, and exercise right, but there is always some rule we're bending or breaking. A book or some organization or some church tells us what we need to do to be a good person, a good mother, a good father, a good whatever. We can't measure up. We can't keep up. But at His birth Jesus provides the only way to resolve the problem of not measuring up and of not keeping up. Without Him we must continue under all this pressure with no end in sight. The truth is that even with faith in Jesus, the most we will do in this life, morally speaking, is just get started at holiness. By the time we die we'll be nowhere near where Jesus was at His birth. In this life, it is enough to know that by faith in Christ, *God is ready to completely accept us now as we actually are.*

Do you know the story of Joseph helping Pharaoh in Genesis 41? It tells us that Pharaoh's "mind was troubled. He sent for all the magicians and wise men of Egypt" (Gen.41:8). Pharaoh told them his dreams, and wanted their help to understand it all, but they could tell him nothing. But Pharaoh's cupbearer told him about a "young Hebrew" he had met in prison. He explained to Pharaoh that this young Hebrew had helped him by explaining the meaning of his dream to him and that he turned out to be amazingly right. Pharaoh says, in effect, "Bring him to me." They bring Joseph up out of the dungeon, clean him up, give him some new clothes, and take him to Pharaoh. When Joseph explains the meaning of the dreams and advises Pharaoh about what he should do, Pharaoh is pleased and asks, "Can we find anyone like this man, one in whom is the spirit of God?" (41:37). There was something very different about Joseph than all of his other advisors, and Pharaoh discerned it. In Joseph, Pharaoh encountered God's own holiness.

Maybe, like Pharaoh, your mind is troubled. Life is just so many bad dreams. Perhaps you anguish over something you have done or have allowed to be done, today, yesterday, or years ago. You have tried everything to deal with your guilt and shame. You have run out of ideas on coping with it, or trouble with your life or with your spouse or your children. You've got some big problems that you cannot figure out. I want to be like Pharaoh's cupbearer. I know someone who can help you. Not Joseph, but Jesus. Figuratively speaking, maybe you've been keeping Him down in the dungeon or wherever you keep your Christmas stuff. It is time to bring Him up, bring Jesus up. Welcome Him into your troubled heart. He wants to give you what only He possesses, and what you can never achieve. Get Him out of the basement or the attic or the little boxes of your thinking, and give Him a place in all the living spaces of your life and mind. His birth is God's way to give holiness back to us. It doesn't solve all of our problems, but it is the first and most important step towards the resolution of our guilt and shame and everything else that is against us. The Apostle Paul says that He "has become for us wisdom from God– that is our righteousness, holiness, and redemption" (1Cor.1:30). Jesus can be *your* righteousness, holiness, and redemption. You can find no one else like Him!

The Donor of holiness, the Holy One, waits for you to call out to Him, no matter what you have done or what has been done to you. Give up your striving, and instead of seeking satisfaction through your own efforts, instead of trusting in yourself, receive this holy standing before God today by calling upon Him. I know a young Hebrew who can help you. Call out to God now and pray, *Bring Him to me!*

The Debt of Jesus's Name

Luke 2:21; Matthew 1:21

> On the eighth day, when it was time to circumcise him, he was named Jesus, the angel had given him before he had been conceived. Luke 2:21

> She will give birth to a son and you are to give Him the name Jesus because He will save His people from their sins. Matthew 1:21

Awhile back, I heard about this 26 year-old woman who won $86 million in the Idaho lottery. In an interview she said, "I have worked hard all my life, and from now on, if I want it, I'll buy it!" I thought that was funny because she was so young, but I understood her joy. She had the credit, she had the cash, she had the *standing* to do now whatever she pleased. She was going on a shopping spree.

In a way, this is how it is with Jesus. By God's own foreordained plan, His only Son was awarded the unenviable and miserable prize of the cross. He suffered and died, but won big when He surprised and flummoxed the world and was raised up from the dead. In His death He had taken upon Himself the debt of our sins, and so paid the price of our redemption. He won victory over sin and death and now He is like someone who has so much and announces to all the world, "If I want it, I'll buy it." We could never pay the price of our sins, but Jesus Christ has *standing*. The unlimited currency of the cross is His to spend.

How did this happen, where did it begin? How did the credit of the cross upon which He died, become so abundant that it could cover me, cover you, cover all who believe? It began on the eighth day of His life at His circumcision. The Apostle Paul tells the Galatians that according to Jewish law "every man that is circumcised is a debtor to the whole law" (Galatians 5:3). In being circumcised, humanly speaking, Christ took upon Himself the requirement to keep God's law for us who could not keep the law and so became a debtor to the law. *He gave His complete obedience to the whole law for my sake.*

At Christmas we often hear what the name of Jesus means for us. But it cannot really be understood unless we know what His name meant for Him. "Nomina debita" is an old Latin phrase that simply means "names are debts." The poet John Donne, says that no one "has a name but that name is legal to him… Our names are debts that we owe to those who know our name." Jesus's name placed Him under a great debt to us if we know His name. He became obligated to give me His name in order to clear my own, so that my name could be written in the Book of Life (Revelation 21:27).

The name "Jesus" contains the root of the Hebrew term "save." It is the Greek form of the Hebrew name "Joshua" which means "Yahweh saves" or "salvation of Yahweh." The name was, in fact, commonly used among the Jews. Perhaps Mary's first-born child was known as Jesus *of Nazareth* if only to distinguish Him from others who bore the same name. Nevertheless, however many bore this name in ancient Palestine, it was never assigned by an angel who spelled out a very specific meaning. When Joseph found out about Mary's pregnancy, he started thinking about putting her away secretly. An angel appeared to him in a dream and told him to give this name to the child and what the name would mean: "He will save His people from their sins." The name "Jesus" would place Him under this obligation, a debt that He willingly and joyfully undertook in order to do something never done before. Simeon describes it:

> For my eyes have seen Your salvation which You have prepared in the sight of all people, a light for revelation to the Gentiles and for glory to your people Israel. Luke 2:30-32

Jesus would accomplish salvation. Why does Simeon think this about Him? It was supernatural. "The Holy Spirit was upon him" (Luke 2:25,26,27). Three times we are told that it was God who showed this to Simeon. At eight days old, all babies sort of look alike, don't they? But God was showing Simeon that this baby was the Son of God and that He would be a light like no other before. Not once, not twice, but three times the work of the Holy Spirit is mentioned by Luke as the source of Simeon's understanding. Maybe today the Holy Spirit is revealing Him to you, too? To most people, all the different ideas about God are like a room full of babies. From a distance, they kind of all look alike. But today perhaps something seems different to you about Jesus and Christianity. Is the Holy Spirit showing you that Jesus is God's only Son and that Christianity is true? Do you wonder why such a thought should cross your mind? How many times is this for you? Is this the first time? The second time? How many times will it take?

There had been light given before, illumination about who God is, but it was mainly for Israel, not all the world, not like this. In the Old Testament, when the name of God is proclaimed we are told, "The Lord is merciful and gracious, patient and abounding in goodness and truth, keeping mercy for thousands, forgiving iniquity and transgression and sin" (Exodus 34:6-7). Why would God describe His goodness and truth as abounding or abundant? Isn't it because He means to be merciful towards us? Yes. To be gracious towards us? Yes. If I turn my life over to Him, doesn't this mean that He has more than enough to take care of me? Yes, He has more than enough. What a great light this is! And now Simeon says that this light is *even greater and more brilliant in Jesus Christ* and "for revelvation to the Gentiles" - for all the world. In being given a name that was a debt, the Son was showing us the heart of the Father. As Jesus says in John 14:9, "Anyone who has seen Me has seen the Father." Such a statement properly considered staggers the mind. God wanted to show His Almighty willingness to take our debts upon Himself in Jesus Christ. So the light of which Simeon speaks here was seen in the Old Testament, but it pales in significance to the light he sees in Jesus.

I have a light on my smart phone, and it is pretty good. If I am in the dark it is very handy to have. But if you were to see me walking down the street in broad daylight using this light, you would wonder: What is wrong with him? I also have a lamp next to my bed. If I wake up in the night, I can turn it on and read. But I don't need these lights when the sun is up. These are all lesser lights. Simeon is saying, in effect, "I've seen *the* Light that gives light to all the world!" In Jesus Christ, the sun is up and brilliant. No other lights are needed.

Beyond the debt of His name there is even more in that He wants you to have. The range of names given to God answers to a catalogue of human needs fulfilled in Jesus. God's name answers to every need we have. Do you need comfort? He is the "God of all comfort" (2Cor.1:3). Do you need peace of conscience? He is the God of

Peace (1Thess.5:23). Do you need direction in life? Are you in the dark right now about which way to go? Are you full of doubt? He is the Father of lights (James1:7). Notice the plural form "lights." God is able to assist and illuminate our various and multiple paths when we turn to Him, whatever it is, wherever we are, and whoever we are. He has a name to answer every objection, every trouble, every heartache. Every aspect of His name is a promise. Name to yourself that one great wrong in your life that you cannot undo. *His name is greater.* Greater than that one trap from which you cannot seem to escape, the one foul thing, the one gross continuing lapse or sin, the one thing that depresses you, frustrates you, the one deep down unhappiness that propels you to the fridge to eat ice cream out of the carton because you're feeling the blues. What is the thing that makes you so mean or difficult to be around, the thing that comes back to your conscience with a blow? Take whatever is, however much it is, from wherever it comes, from the past, from the present, plus the dread of any future failure, and place it all alongside the matchless name, the name of Jesus – the name with a debt, a debt that He has paid. If you have a broken heart, and if you have a searching mind, and look to Him, you will find that He will make His truth and power and mercy relevant to your every need. He is our Redeemer, our Savior, our Shield, our Rock, our Strength, our Almighty. This name, *Jesus*, is our Salvation, our Righteousness, our Wisdom, our Truth, our Way, our Lamb, our Lion, our Love, our Groom, our Star. May the power of His Holy Spirit, not once, not twice, but three times, even a thousand times, supernaturally show you and fill you just as Simeon was shown and filled, with the joyous certainty of this Name that cannot be overdrawn, overworked, or overextended - the name of the Son of God. The name, *Jesus*, a debt for our sins taken by Him, paid in full by Him, a name that He keeps to this day for our sake.

His Father's House
Luke 2:49

> Why is it that you were looking for Me? Did you not know that I had to be in My Father's house? Luke 2:49

In a very old book there is a paragraph about a young boy who would grow up to alter the course of history in a way that no one ever expected. In the book, *Plutarch's Lives,* the ancient historian, Plutarch, explains that even as a child, Alexander the Great seemed to know who he was and demonstrated how great he would be someday. Persian ambassadors came to the court of Philip of Macedonia, and they met Philip's son, young prince Alexander. It was expected that the boy would be fascinated by their Persian dress and appearance. But when he was introduced, he showed little interest in their clothes or appearance or rank. Instead he asked them, "How do you build your roads through the mountains of your land?" He asked them questions about their land's borders and geography. He wanted to know how their king treated his enemies after he had subdued them. Even then, it seems, he was thinking about his future campaigns of conquest. The Persians were astonished by the intellect and insight of the young boy who, in a few short years and at the age of just sixteen, would begin his conquest of the world. He knew who he was. The Persians they would have been wise on that very day to bow down and surrender to him, then and there.

Jesus Knew Who He Was

> After three days they found Him in the temple courts, sitting among the teachers, listening to them and asking them

questions. Everyone was amazed at His understanding and His answers. Luke 2:46-47

Here is another brief paragraph about a boy who would grow up to alter the course of a miserable world's history; who, as a perfect human being living among people, opened the doors of the house of Almighty God's wisdom and said to all the world, "Come in!" Luke's gospel wants the world to believe in Him.

Luke's point is that Jesus, from an early age, knew who He was. He understood His unique relationship to God, and this summoned in Him a devotion to God's purposes that exceeded even His closest family relationships. He did not become the Messiah later on. He was not chosen by God from among others. He was at birth the Son of God, and He grew up knowing it. As the Son of God He had to follow His calling, even if it meant trouble and misunderstanding. This prepares us for what is coming next in the life of the Son of God as Luke tells His story to us. Likewise, if you are a follower of Jesus, when you know who you are and understand God's purposes for your life, it will put you at odds not only with the world, but with your closest friends, and even your own family. Maybe you're married to someone who isn't a Christian or maybe you are in a work situation or some other setting with people who do not really understand you. Knowing who you are will sometimes bring trouble into your life. Do we know who we are? Jesus knew who He was.

He Also Worked at Being Who He Was

> Everyone was amazed at His understanding and His answers. Luke 2:47

We have seen previously in this chapter how Joseph and Mary did everything according to Jewish law. Luke probably includes this story here so that Gentile readers understand that the Jewish leadership, who later rejected Jesus and had Him crucified, did not do so because He was some kind of outsider. Jesus took His Jewish responsibilities very seriously.

Jesus worked at understanding His fully human responsibilities as a true Israelite, and this meant knowing the Hebrew Bible. Luke says: "Jesus grew in wisdom and stature and in favor with God and men" (Luke 2:52). Elsewhere, it tells us He intentionally limited Himself: "He did not count equality with God a thing to be grasped but emptied Himself, taking the form of a servant" (Philippians 2:6-7). He made Himself a servant, and servants must work. He had the complete personality of God but limited His power to know all. He had to grow in wisdom, just as He grew physcially. His understanding of Moses, the Prophets, and all the writings of the Old Testament was something at which He worked diligently. He probably had certain parts of Scripture that He went back to again and again and favorite passages or verses that He memorized. Luke says that after His resurrection Jesus met up with two of His disciples outside Emmaus. "Beginning with Moses and the Prophets, He explained to them what was said in all the Scriptures concerning Himself" (Luke 24:27). They walked along with Him and said later: "Were not our hearts burning within us while He talked with us on the road and opened the Scriptures to us?" (Luke 2:32). That is why, if you believe and are a follower of Jesus, you study the Bible, prepare Bible studies, or go to Bible studies. You're wanting to walk with Him, too. You are guided by that same kind of burning heart. You find in Him, and from Him, the energy that makes you want to work at who you are, just as He did.

He Is Determined that Others Know Who He Is

> Your father and I have been anxiously searching for you. Why is it that you were looking for me? Did you not know that <u>I had to be in My Father's house?</u> Luke 2:48-49

He isn't simply speaking about the psychological value of having God as a father figure in His life. He really knew that God was His Father, and He lived and acted on that basis. Jesus came from a good Jewish home. Joseph filled the role of an earthly father, but Jesus's heart and soul belonged to God alone. The presence of a young boy in the midst of Israel's great teachers was not in and of itself extraordinary. The teachers of the law often gave public lectures near the Passover, and young boys would listen, sometimes ask questions. The age of 12 was the age at which a young Jewish boy would become what is described in other literature as "a Son of the Law."

But there is even more going on here in Luke's particular expression, "had to be." It is from the Greek term "dei" meaning "necessary," and it is translated "had to be" or as NIV translates, "must be." Jesus didn't speak Greek, but Aramaic. Luke purposefully uses this Greek term to render what Jesus said that day, and on many other occasions. It is used throughout His life and ministry to describe the direction of His heart and soul, His sacrifice and suffering. In Luke 9:22 He says, "The Son of Man <u>must</u> suffer many things, and be rejected by the elders and chief priests and scribes, and be killed, and be raised up on the third day." He had to suffer (c.f. 17:25 24:26, 44,46, Acts 3:21, 17:3). He had to keep going. In Luke 13:31-33, some Pharisees say to Him, "Go away and depart from here, for Herod wants to kill You." Jesus answered: "I must keep going..." He had to suffer for *us*. He had to keep going for *us*. Why? In John

14:31, when He is about to go to His death on the cross, He explains that "the world must learn that I love the Father and that I do exactly what my Father has commanded Me." In a way, it is the strength of Jesus's love for God that leads Him to the cross and saves me, and everyone who puts their trust in Him. He loves us, yes, but His love for the Father motivated Him to sacrifice and suffer and keep going all His life, all the way from Bethlehem to Calvary. The writer of Hebrews says, "Let us fix our eyes on Jesus, the author and perfecter of our faith, who <u>for the joy</u> set before Him endured the cross scorning its shame and sat down at the right hand of the throne of God" (Hebrews 12:2). If we have any real joy it is because of the joy He pursued in making Himself known, in handing Himself over for us and in suffering for us.

On that day in the temple stood the conquerer of the world in juvenile form, surrounded by Judaism's highest spiritual ambassadors. Maybe these very same teachers would be among those who would later gnash their teeth and plan to kill Jesus. Standing in their midst was the One who could alter the course of their lives, my life, your life, any life! Before them was a spiritual Alexander who would conquer all the nations of the world, not by the sword and war, but by His sacrifice and word. Born King of kings and Lord of Lords, He knows all the roads and borders of humanity, and is able to triumph no matter what lies in His way. Perhaps Gamaliel or Caiaphas, the great teachers of Moses, were present that day. They would have been wise to bow down and surrender to Him, right then and there! But they didn't. Through the power of the Holy Spirit, He stands before *you* now. Decide what you will do!

The Christmas Bell

Luke 2:13-14

> Suddenly, a great company of the heavenly host appeared with the angel, praising God and saying, "Glory to God in the highest, and on earth peace on whom His favor rests." Luke 2:13-14

A few years ago, in a remarkable story of perseverance, a young a woman fell off the shrimp boat she was working on during rough seas in the Gulf of Mexico. No one heard her cry out after she had gone overboard, and her boat soon disappeared on the horizon. She was 70 miles away from the nearest land with no life preserver. She didn't know what to do except to start swimming, so she swam, through the afternoon, into the dusk, and then the dusk turned into darkness, and she swam. Sometime during the night when exhaustion was overwhelming her, there all alone in the endless darkness of the ocean, she thought she heard a bell. Yes, there it was again, a bell, she was sure of it. She started swimming toward the sound, stopping to tread water, waiting to hear it again. As she swam toward it, she had to struggle because the current would carry her away from the sound, but the sound of the bell would help her find her way back on course. And so she swam toward the bell all through the night. Just as dawn was breaking on the Gulf, as she struggled to stay above the waves, she saw it – an offshore oil rig with a metal ladder on the side and a bell sounding. Exhausted, she swam for all her life, made it to the rig, and was rescued that day.

We may not realize it or act like it, but it is the gospel truth that we are lost and treading water in a vast sea far from land. What I mean is that recognizing you are in need of salvation is like realizing that you are in an ocean without a chance of surviving. Our sins, like waves, will eventually overwhelm us. You might know the story of the human race, as the Bible tells it, and about the fall of Adam and Eve. We, along with them- all humanity -went overboard and were lost. In the beginning, humanity rebelled against God. We have been swimming around in circles and struggling ever since. Most of us are very tired. We are all about to sink. Christmas is the sounding of a bell.

In our reading, the angel and the heavenly host are praising God. This deserves some reflection. In heaven the angels praise God as their Creator. He created them along with all of creation, and they lead all creation in praising Him: "Glory to God in the highest," they shout. But what else do they say? "And on earth peace on whom His favor rests." God is our Creator, too, but now He is revealed in Jesus Christ as our *Redeemer* - the One who can rescue us from our peril. The angels circle the throne in praise. We, on the other hand, are circling the drain. Our rescue thus prompts an even greater and more glorious praise than the angels could ever offer to God. The bell of salvation has sounded, and praise, like the angels of heavens could never offer, is about to begin.

To hear that bell, to understand what the gospel means, changes us. In Ephesians 4:1 the Apostle Paul explains what a Christian's life should be like. He says, "Be completely humble and gentle." Why does that ring so true? Because of Jesus. Later in His life, after His family found Him in the temple, we are told that Jesus "went down to Nazareth with them and was obedient to them" (Luke 2:50-52). This is a theme in the life of Jesus. In John 6:38 He says, "I have come down from heaven not to do my will but to do the will of Him who sent me." He led a downward kind of life. He was often headed *down*. His obedience to God required it. He was humble. This was not the beginning of His humility and obedience, was it? No, it began before this. Before Bethlehem, it began in heaven. As we read in Philippians 2:6-11: "…being in very nature God [Jesus] did not think equality with God something to be grasped but made Himself nothing." Jesus Christ deliberately veiled His glory in human flesh so that there would be no outward indication to anyone of His true rank and status. Like we sing in the carol: "Mild He lays His glory by…born that men no more may die." Before the angel appeared to Mary or spoke to Joseph or frightened a shepherd and his sheep, before Jesus was born in the stable, before the first wise man got on his camel to follow the star so that he could find Him in Bethlehem, before all of that, Jesus made Himself nothing.

What about us? What should we make of ourselves? What are you making of yourself when you are upset or angry about how someone is treating you or acting towards you? Do you perhaps feel this way because you've made too much of yourself? Your ego, your selfishness has you going round in circles. Stop and listen for the bell. Are you pulled off and pulled away by how others treat you, or by the currents and trends around you? In the darkness of this world, has God given you ears to hear the Christmas bell? Swim for the bell, swim for the Son of God, swim for Bethlehem. Can you hear it? Humble yourself, swim for the downward kind of life before you really do go down, swim for the Savior born to you, swim for the baby born in Bethlehem, the Man in heaven who threw Himself overboard for your sake. At Bethlehem the light is breaking. Swim for it!

A Savior for the Stress of Our Sin

Mark 1:32-45

> Jesus replied, "Let us go somewhere else – to the nearby villages- so that I can preach there also. That is why I have come." Mark 1:38

Jesus reveals something important to us in Mark 1:38. His ministry in the world was always connected to the fact that He had *come from God*. He related His teaching ministry to the eternal purpose, to the Divine mission, for which He had been sent and for which He had come from God. Consider what He says elsewhere:

> I came from God and now am here. I have not come on My own; but He sent Me. John 8:42

> I came from the Father and entered the world; now I am leaving the world and going back to the Father. John 16:28

Because of the monumental responsibility He carried, Jesus probably lived about the most stressful life you could ever imagine. It wasn't stress like ours - stress mixed with sin - but it was stress. His life was filled with stress.

The Stress of God's Love

> People brought to Jesus all the sick and demon-possessed. The whole town gathered at the door. Mark 1:32-40

Imagine having the power to heal anyone of any kind of disease. Imagine having the perfect undiluted compassion of God. Imagine being surrounded by disease and sickness everywhere you went. Imagine, though, that healing people is not why you are here. That is a recipe for stress. The pressure upon Jesus was tremendous with the constant needs of people; no time to eat, no time to rest, no time to think. He had to get away just to think and pray.

> Very early in the morning ... Jesus got up, left the house and went off to a solitary place to pray. Mark 1:35

Jesus had a priority. The purpose for which He came was not to perform healings. All the sickness, disease, poverty, ignorance, and abuse in this world is not the problem. They are symptoms, signs, and consequences of the problem which is sin. That is what Jesus came to do something about. The problem is that the human race does not have the character to match its achievements. It does have the character to match its scientific or medical accomplishments. It does not have the character to match its educational accomplishments. It does not have the character to match its political accomplishments. We do not have the character to match our sociological accomplishments. We do not have the character to match our artistic accomplishments. We do not have the character to match our athletic accomplishments. Humanity has a problem of *character - a disease of the heart and will.* Consider these passages:

> We all like sheep have gone astray, each of us has turned to his own way. Isaiah 53:6

> There is no one righteous, not even one. Romans 3:10

> All have sinned and fall short of the glory of God. Romans 3:23

What if Jesus had just spent His few years of ministry healing everyone that He could touch? How many lives could He have improved?! It would have been a remarkable period in Israel and perhaps the entire Middle East. But Jesus knew that healing was not enough, that is not why He had come. He came to die for us.

I get so stressed out in life. You know how it is to be stressed out, trying to decide what to do. What school to go to or what job to seek, or who to help or how to help. Families get stressed out. How do we pay our bills? Which child needs our attention? How do we decide who should get braces and who should not? How do you handle this or that conflict in your home? How do you balance work with your relationship to your husband or wife? The church gets stressed out. Trustees stress over the building. Who is going to lock up, or turn the lights off? The deacons stress over helping people, picking people up, getting lunch ready for hundreds of people. The elders stress over how to shepherd the church and how to care for the ministries. These things are stressful. Thank God that we can go to Him and get direction! Thank God that the Savior took care of my sin for me so that I can always have hope if I trust Him. I NEVER HAVE TO BE STRESSED OUT OVER MY SIN AGAIN. I may need to repent. I may be disappointed in myself. I may need to go to Him or come to you for forgiveness. I may need to mature. I may need to mend. I may need wisdom. I may go broke. I may get into all kinds of trouble and messes in life. But Jesus underwent great stress in going to the cross to give His life for me, and He settled the most stressful problem of my life so that I could be restored in my relationship to God for all eternity. In our text, that is why Jesus wants to go into the surrounding towns to preach and teach. That is His priority. On the way He meets a leper.

The Stretch of God's Love

> A man with leprosy came to him and begged Him on his knees. "If You are willing, You can make me clean." Filled with compassion, Jesus reached out His hand and touched the man, "I am willing," He said, "Be clean." Mark 1:40-42

The leper, like everyone, knows that Jesus is in the vicinity and goes to find Him. We know from the description of leprosy in Leviticus 13 and 14 that this is a variety of infectious skin diseases. The term describes peeling, scaling, or scabbing. But in the OT the term describes not so much a specific disease but a class of people.

The idea of excluding lepers from society as practiced in the Old Testament is often understood as a kind of public health policy, but in fact, in the ancient world we don't find this understanding. 2 Kings 5:1 tells us of Naaman, captain of Syrian army. He was a leper but did his work and moved about society freely, even conversing with the King of Syria. Lepers were *not* automatically cut off from society in the ancient world. We know from other Rabbinical sources that strangers and soujourners were exempt from the Levitical regulation and so the question arises, why exactly was the exclusion from society in the Old Testament limited to Israelites? The answer must be that the Levitical law that put the leper out of the camp was not a health policy, but a religious one. It says, "If ...the man is indeed infected with a skin disease and is unclean. The priest must pronounce him ceremonially unclean" (Lev. 13:44). Leprosy seems to have been a sickness in Israel that taught people something about God and themselves. God chose leprosy as the disease to teach people by ceremony, image, and practice that He could have nothing to do with *sin*. The temporary cutting off of the leper demonstrated how sin cut them off from God. But the restoration of a leper showed the purifying power of God *over sin*. The leper was considered as dead. He bore all the signs of death – separation from people and torn up garments (Lev.13:45). Restoration involved the same elements used for those who had touched a dead body, like cedarwood, hyssop, and scarlet (Num.19:6,13,18, Lev.14:4-7).

In our text, a leper comes and falls down before Jesus, "If You are willing, You can make me clean." Notice Jesus's response to the leper: "The Lord was moved with compassion…" The God who would not, could not, permit a leper in the camp where He dwelt; the God who could have nothing to do with death, is overcome by the sight. He stretches out His hand over the chasm of death and hell and touches death. "I am willing, be cleansed."

The miracles gave the people who witnessed them or experienced them - and give all those who read about them today - a challenge: Decide what your response will be to Jesus and His claims about who He is. If you are already a believer, the response He seeks is for you to trust Him when your plans get interrupted, when things become sressful. Jesus has His priorities, but He is also able to respond with compassion to the needs around Him. Some of the greatest moments of His ministry are when He is interrupted going somewhere to do something else. Maybe you have experienced an interruption during your day or your travels or during your favorite Korean drama. Someone may not fall down before you, but it is a need. Maybe God has put this need or this person right there in front of you in order to ask you, "Are you willing?" Sin made us all lepers, cut off from Him in spiritual death. Maybe you have heard this question before: "I asked Jesus, 'How much do you love me?' And

Jesus said, 'This much.' Then He stretched out His arms and died." Because His love was stretched out for me, my life is not now my own, but His.

The Strictness of God's Love

> Jesus sent him away with a strong warning … don't tell this to anyone. Mark 1:43-45

Jesus has great compassion but He doesn't want the man to talk about Him – not a word to anyone, because He has not yet gone to cross. This is not for us today! Now He commands us to go out and tell everyone. The cross has changed everything. There is a wideness in God's mercy, but a strictness in His love. I don't mean strict and overbearing, I mean *He wants His love strictly associated with the cross*. We might be excited about Jesus but until we know about the cross we're not ready to talk about Him. The Apostle Paul was strict about this. "I did not come with eloquence or superior wisdom …For I resolved to know nothing while I was with you except Jesus Christ and Him crucified" (1 Corinthians 2:2). Jesus did not want His miracles to stand *apart* from the cross. He had to be stretched out on the cross so that we could be touched by the hand of salvation. Hear this all you stressed out sheep gone astray! The Shepherd has come to care for us. He endured great stress to do this for us. Now He is alive forevermore. Hear this, all you moral lepers cut off from God! You do not need to live cut-off from God. Jesus has come for you. Do you think you might need Him? Then bow down to Him now and ask Him, "Are you willing?" The gospel has three words for you: Yes, He is!

The Mighty Power of Forgiveness

Mark 2:1-12

The Apostle Paul summarizes God's redemptive work in Romans 5:8: "But God demonstrates His own love for us in this: While we were still sinners, Christ died for us." We do not have to try to be good enough (nor could we) so that we can earn the forgiveness God offers. If we have received Christ (or receive Him now) as the Son of God, we have that forgiveness along with all its signs.

The Message of Forgiveness

> So many gathered that there was no room left, not even outside the door, and He preached the word to them. Mark 2:2

Jesus, it says in our text, "preached the word to them." And that word was the glorious message of God's forgiveness for all who would repent and turn to Him. People are drawn to that message today just as they were drawn to Him in this scene from Mark's gospel.

Whatever our own ideas about forgiveness might be, the Bible views forgiveness as a Mighty Power. The proclamation of the gospel by Jesus was, and is today, a life-changing, a life-altering message. Something far greater than a wiping of the slate is meant by "forgiveness." Although that is part of it and a genuine human need.

I saw a handwritten sign recently posted at an intersection near where I live:

> Dear woman in the nice black car, I totally overreacted and I'm sorry. I've almost been hit so many times while walking through this intersection that when you didn't give me the right of way I flipped. Not cool and not how people should treat each other. I feel stupid about my end of things and I'm truly <u>sorry.</u>   Sincerely, Me

This is good but what God does is far greater. Our idea about forgiveness is but a slight, faint shadow, considering what God does. Adam and Eve's response when confronted with their sin in the book of Genesis was to fear God. They hid (Genesis 3:8)! And their sin, our sin, required greater power than the very creation of the universe. God spoke creation into existence, saying, "Let there be light." In Psalm 8:3 the psalmist describes God's creation as "the work of Your fingers." But when Adam and Eve sinned God could not simply say, "Let there be forgiveness." He does not say, "Well, it's okay, I forgive you." Because of His holiness, and in order to forgive us, *a greater power was needed than the power that created the world.* About this power, Isaiah 52:10 says, "The Lord will lay bare His holy arm in the sight of all nations, and all the ends of the earth will see the salvation of our God."

God made the heavens with His fingers, but forgiveness required His bare sweaty almighty arm. God had to roll up His sleeves to save us. Ephesians 1:7 says, "In Him we have redemption through His blood, *the forgiveness of sins.*" In Colossians 1:13 he says, "For He rescued us from the dominion of darkness and brought us into the kingdom of the Son He loves, in whom we have *the forgiveness of sins.*" This salvation is a change of life, a change of character, a change of heart, a change of master. You might say you follow Jesus, but if He is not your Lord, then you are not forgiven of your sins! For those who turn to Him, FORGIVEN is the final irrevocable verdict of the last day, the Day of Judgment. Jesus was offering that to His listeners. He offers it on earth HERE AND NOW.

The Controversy Over Forgiveness

> Some men came, bringing to Him a paralytic, carried by the four of them. Mark 2:3

This message creates controversy. Look at what happens. These men come carrying someone who is paralyzed. There is no room even outside the door, but it doesn't stop them. Maybe they asked people to move or tried to get in some other way. Nothing worked. But here are *four guys* (a.k.a. men who can do anything with duct tape) No one is restraining them. One of them says, "I've got an idea! Let's just go through the roof!" The text says literally that they "unroofed the roof."

It seems like a bad idea to tear up someone's roof, but their belief that Jesus could heal this man is so strong, they're willing to be a little reckless. They lower him down:

> When Jesus saw their faith, he said to the paralytic, "Son, your sins are forgiven." Mark 2:5

His words must have seemed strange. I doubt that this is what the man on the mat is thinking he would hear: "Son, your sins are forgiven." Don't misunderstand this. His sins are not the reason for His paralysis. That would be "folk religion" which Jesus refutes elsewhere. In John 9:2-3 His disciples ask about the blind man, "who sinned, this man or his parents? Neither … said Jesus, this happened so that the work of God might be displayed in his life." Now the controversy begins.

Don't be too hard on these teachers of the law. They are correct: Who can forgive sins but God alone? Only God has such power. The bare arm of God must be revealed. Jesus has come with that power to grant to us FORGIVENESS FROM GOD. Jesus knows what the teachers of the law are thinking, and He says, in effect, "I will show you, right now, who I am. I will show you the authority that I can and will forgive sins." Jesus sees this man's and his friends' faith in Him. He heals him. We should note exactly why this happens according to the text: "That you may know that the Son of Man has authority on earth to forgive sins… I tell you, get up, take up your mat and walk."

The Signs of Forgiveness

> "But that you may know that the Son of Man has authority on earth to forgive sins," He said to the paralytic, "I tell you, get up, take up your mat, and walk." Mark 2:10-11

Look at the signs of forgiveness. "He got up, took his mat, and walked out in full view of them all." He is instantly and fully and amazingly restored. For this man the sign that his sins were forgiven was his miraculous healing. For us today the sign of forgiveness that we are given is the presence of the Holy Spirit working in our lives: "Having believed you were marked in Him with a seal, the promised Holy Spirit" (Eph.1:13). In this man's restoration we see a tremendous spiritual truth, a picture of the new heart and mind that are ours in Christ.

This is what the forgiveness of sins means, that your heart can be made new. It means your life can be changed. It means restoration. It means the power to get up from whatever is paralyzing you, to walk away from whatever has diminished you, to overcome whatever has reduced you to the crippled, perplexed, whining, fearful, distrustful, suspicious, vengeful, wicked, nasty, little person that you are when you are under the power of sin and the devil. God gives you the power to walk in new life, to put off the old and put on the new (Eph. 4:22), to overcome and to no longer be under the dominion of sin (Rom.6:14).

Paul spells out the remarkable change with the expression "some of you were" when writing to the Corinthians.

> Do you not know that the wicked will not inherit the kingdom of God? Do not be deceived; Neither the sexually immoral nor idolaters nor adulterers nor male prostitutes nor homosexual offenders nor thieves nor the greedy nor drunkards nor slanderers nor swindlers will inherit the kingdom of God. And that is what some of you were. But you were washed, you were sanctified, you were justified in the name of the Lord Jesus Christ and by the Spirit of God." 1 Corinthians 6:9-11.

The forgiveness of sins is a mighty power. It is a cleansing, washing, sanctifying, justifying, power that is demonstrated by the Spirit of God. It was demonstrated by Jesus in the gospels through the healings and miracles. The lame walked. The blind received their sight. Lepers were made clean.

Now, for us, the sign of forgiveness is the presence of the Holy Spirit. People are turned, changed, washed, sanctified, and justified. The forgiveness of sins takes you out of the dominion of darkness and brings you into the kingdom of God's Son.

Maybe you are here today and like the man that Jesus healed, it probably seems strange to think that what you need is the forgiveness of your sins. You have your health that you are worried about. You have bills that worry you. You have a job that you are worried about. You have some house or project or troubled relationship that you are worried about. You have so many kinds of problems, and your friends invited you here today. They picked you up in their car and brought you here or maybe met up with you just outside. It is just as if you had been carried in here on a stretcher or a mat. Maybe you wonder, "Can Jesus help me?" Jesus addresses the paralytic as a "son." The term indicates he was probably a young man. Maybe you are such a young man or woman. You are not paralyzed physically but maybe life is so difficult that you feel like you have no power to move, no power to go on, no power to change yourself or your circumstances.

If you could ask that man, the one Jesus healed, what really matters, I think he would tell you that he knows now how much it meant to have his sins forgiven. "It was the greatest day of my life," he might say, "being healed so that I could walk, but eventually I grew old and died. I have been in heaven and glory now for over two thousand years! I learned on that day that I had a greater need than healing. I needed my sins forgiven. I hope that in reading about me in Mark's Gospel, *you* will learn that is true, too."

Lifelong Patients

Mark 2:13-17

> When the teachers of the law who were Pharisees saw Him eating with "sinners" and tax collectors, they asked His disciples: "Why does He eat with tax collectors and sinners?" On hearing this Jesus said to them, "It is not the healthy who need a doctor, but the sick. I have not come to call the righteous, but sinners." Mark 2:16-17

As noted previously, the Apostle Paul summarizes God's redemptive plan in Romans 5:8- "But God demonstrates His own love for us in this: While we were still sinners, Christ died for us." We do not have to try to be good enough (nor could we!) so that we can earn that forgiveness. As we have seen previously in Mark 2:1-12, Jesus heals the paralytic as a sign to confirm to everyone watching that He has the power to forgive sins and that the forgiveness of sins is a truly mighty power. Like the man who was paralyzed and was completely healed (Mark 2:1-12), we were once "paralyzed" by sin but by faith in Jesus are spiritually healed so that we might "walk" in the power of the Holy Spirit. Forgiveness is a mighty healing power. Jesus refers to Himself as having such power in Mark 2:17: "It is not the healthy who need a doctor but the sick."

The Doctor Who Can Heal Us

> Once again Jesus went out beside the lake. A large crowd came to Him, and He began to teach them. Mark 2:13

The teaching of Jesus Christ on the Kingdom of God, and on repentance and faith, was a marvelous tonic, like nothing anyone had ever tasted before. People were drinking it down. It was such marvelous news! In Chapter 2 and up to verse 17, Mark is focusing on Jesus's power and authority to forgive sins. No doubt this was a central part of His teaching. The healing of the paralytic in the previous verses has shown His power to forgive in the most astonishing way. A man is miraculously healed.

Whatever our own ideas about forgiveness might be, the Bible views forgiveness as an extremely mighty power. The proclamation of the gospel by Jesus was, and is today, a life-changing message. Our ideas about forgiveness are slight, a faint shadow, in light of what God does when He forgives. It is greater than a pardon, greater than a wiping clean of the slate. It is a change of life and a change of character. This is made clear in the next verse.

The Patients Who Need Him

> As He walked along, He saw Levi son of Alphaeus sitting at the tax collector's booth. 'Follow Me,' Jesus told him, and Levi got up and followed Him. Mark 2:14

Consider Levi and you'll understand the patients who need Him. By all measurements of his society, Levi (Matthew), was a corrupt civil servant, a very "sick" man. If grades were being given to all of humanity, tax collectors like Levi were near the bottom of the class, probably assigned a grade of "F" or possibly, a "D."

Degraded and **D**ishonest. Tax collectors overcharged people. They took bribes from the rich and extorted the poor.

Disqualified. Tax collectors were not allowed to give testimony as witnesses because no one trusted them.

Disloyal. Though he was Jewish, a tax collector was considered a traitor because he worked for the hated Romans. He had turned his back on his family, his nation and his God.

Detested. Jewish people despised tax collectors more than Roman officials or soldiers.

Disgraced. By extension, Levi's family would also have been ostracized by the community. He was a letdown to his family and the source of shame.

Defiled. He was considered an outcast, excommunicated from the synagogue.

Choosing Levi as a disciple surely put Jesus's movement at risk. Jesus calls *him*. If you were with Jesus, this is not the guy you would want Jesus to choose as your colleague. Imagine the angels watching all this nearby, shouting as loudly as they shouted praises on the night of His birth, "Wait, no, not him, not him, don't choose him! LORD, STEP AWAY FROM THAT SINNER, PLEASE DO NOT CHOOSE HIM!" From the world's perspective, Levi was a risky choice. *You* were a risky choice. Patients are like him, like us, we look like bad risks, but notice:

1. Jesus has freedom and power to choose whomever He will. As powerful as they seem, powerful figures in our world are not really free to do as they please. Even the greatest powers, kings, and presidents, have constraints. But Jesus really has sovereign *free* will.

It says in Mark 2:14, "As He walked along, He saw Levi." He didn't simply notice Him, He *chose* him. *Follow Me,* Jesus says. This is not really an invitation, like, "Won't you follow Me?" It is more. It is a command but one that brings with it the capacity, strength, power, and *desire* to obey. The gospel asks of us something we cannot do but which it empowers us to do: *To follow Jesus* no matter who you are. He has the freedom to choose you, to change you, and to charge you. *Follow Me.* Paul marvels over this in one of his letters.

> Think of what you were when you were called. Not many of you were wise by human standards; not many were influential; not many were of noble birth. But God chose the foolish things of the world to shame the wise; God chose the weak things of the world to shame the strong. He chose the lowly things of this world and the despised things – and the things that are not – to nullify the things that are so that no one may boast before Him.
> 1Cor.1:26-29

2. Jesus is free to *choose* whomever He will. He also has the freedom and power to *change* whomever He will. What happens when Jesus speaks to Him? Mark 2:14 says, "Levi got up." Mark is intentionally mirroring the previous healing of the paralytic in Mark 2:12: "He got up." Whatever preparation that had been done by the Spirit of God, the result here is no less astonishing than the healing of the paralytic. He shows us instant, complete, and radical change. Luke's account says he "left everything" (Luke 5:28). Jesus has the power to change us.

This is what it means for Him to be Lord of my life. He has chosen me and changed me and charged me. Now I need to *follow Him.* Paul puts it powerfully this way: "I have been crucified with Christ and I no longer live but Christ lives in me. The life I live in the body, I live by faith in the Son of God who loved Me and gave Himself up for me" (Gal. 2:20). He chooses us and changes us and charges us now to serve Him with our whole and complete being.

Have you heard the story of the chicken and the pig who were in their car driving down the road? They passed a sign for an IHOP advertising its breakfast special: Ham and Eggs – $4.95. The chicken looked over at the sign and said, "That's our whole contribution to society: breakfast food!" The pig shook his head, "Look, maybe for you it's a contribution, but for me it's more of a total commitment."

Our Lord's commitment was total, and now we're called and empowered to go "whole hog" – no reservations, no holding nothing back. "In view of God's mercy," Paul says in Romans 12:1, "offer your bodies as living sacrifices to God." What does He ask you to "get up" from? Are you stuck in some lifestyle or habit that is wrong? Levi left the lifestyle of a crook and went on to write the Gospel of Matthew. What does this mean for you? Maybe "getting up" means changing some things, leaving some things, ignoring some things, turning away from some things. I don't know, but I can tell you that you're the kind of patient the Great Physician can help, and He has important work for you to do.

The Hospital We're In (i.e. the church)

> While Jesus was having dinner at Levi's house, many tax collectors and "sinners" were eating with Him and His disciples, for there were many who followed Him…I have not come to call the righteous but sinners. Mark 2:15-17

This passage can appear as an encouragement for us to hang out and socialize with unbelievers, to mix it up with those on the margins, which we should do. But a closer examination of this gathering at Levi's house indicates that they were mostly followers of Jesus. It says that "there were many who followed Him." These were not unbelievers, but people who had been chosen and changed. What we have here is a picture of the church, not the world. In this scene we see what the church is, essentially. There are two, and really only two, essentials.

First, in order to be a member of the church *we have to experience the forgiveness of our sins* as these people did in Levi's house. We need Christ's forgiveness, His absolution. A new life had begun for those at Levi's house. They had become children of their heavenly Father through Jesus. Like them, we need the new life that comes through knowing our sins are forgiven.

Second, *we have to be brought into fellowship with others* as these were brought together in the house church of Levi. If we are now living in a relationship with God, we need to be in relationship with others who have experienced this same forgiveness of sins through Jesus Christ.

It is an intimate fellowship, in which the patients are being restored in their relationship to God and to one another. This is a picture of the primitive and true church. Our fellowship, no matter how many people gather here, must always have a pattern of church life that has obvious equivalency with the essentials we see here. We have to know that our sins are forgiven, and we have to be in relationship with others who have experienced this, too.

Look at the comments of the Pharisees in verse 16, "Why does He eat with tax collectors and sinners?" In the Pharisees view, God's all-loving will was contained and expressed in His holy law and any intimate table fellowship was directed and controlled by this single consideration alone: *obedience to the law*. The church, under their leadership, would not be a hospital for the broken but a health club for the fit. For Jesus, and for the New Testament church, however, God's all loving will was now revealed in Jesus Christ and in the gospel. Intimate table fellowship was directed and controlled by this single consideration: *obedience to the gospel alone*.

The Feast in the House of Levi or *Christ in the House of Levi* is a 1573 Paolo Veronese painting. It is huge, the largest canvas of the 16th century, 18'x41'. Its history is interesting. Originally, it was called *The Last Supper*. The Roman Catholic authorities were taken aback and upset by Veronese's masterpiece. He was asked to explain why the painting contained "buffoons, drunken Germans, dwarfs and other such scurrilities" as well as extravagant, outlandish costumes and settings, in what appeared to be a fantasy version of a Venetian patrician feast. They wanted it redone. Veronese was instructed by the church to change the painting within three months. He thought about it, and instead of altering the painting, Veronese decided to just change the title. *The Last Supper* became *The Feast in the House of Levi*. After this, no more was said.

When you trust in Christ, He gives you a new name, a new title. You might look similar and seem the same, but something remarkable has happened. The Master of All Creation has the power to do this. You are His work. No more is said. Like Veronese' painting, this is huge!

Maybe you are here today, and you wonder, have I been called by Jesus to follow Him? I believe the answer is "yes." Jesus came so that you could be called. Even though He is not physically present now, He is present in the power of the Holy Spirit, and He calls you to follow Him. Believe in Him. Entrust yourself to Him. Maybe you are already one of His followers, but you're not feeling too well as a patient. His patients struggle and mourn and are broken-hearted over their sin. Even at their best, they will break God's law in thought, word, and deed. Take heart, the church is our Lord's hospital. It is not a health club. He expects and understands that we're not just a little out of shape, but we are sick. Ongoing sin, struggles, lapses, and downright foolishness, are not beyond His care. Gross and revolting sin is not beyond His forgiveness and care.

Christ's commitment as our doctor needs to be seen in the light of what we know about the practice of medicine in His time. There were no antibiotics and one single sickness could bring lifelong hardship. Physicians treated their patients *for life*. In dealing with the brokenness of sin, we need Jesus as our Physician for life. We are life-long patients of Jesus Christ. He has called you and gotten you up to follow Him. Now you'll need to continue to consult Him on every matter. Go to Him with every transgression and discover what a wonderful Savior He is. Jesus is ready to help you with all of the symptoms of our current mortality. Some of your spiritual illnesses He will completely heal. He will halt the progress of others, and in some, He will lessen their pain or give you courage to turn away and to withstand. Whatever the trouble, there is healing and help in Him, and He will treat you with all of His tender mercies.

Discipled By Grace

Mark 2:18-22

> Some people came and asked Jesus, "How is it that John's disciples and the disciples of the Pharisees are fasting, but yours are not?" Mark 2:18

One of the most important things the early Christians had to grapple with was the role of the Old Testament law in their lives. These verses teach us about the new and glorious freedom we have as disciples of Jesus Christ and what our relationship is now to the law. The Apostle Paul sums up the entire matter in Galatians 2:16- "A man is not justified by observing the law but by faith in Jesus Christ." The Pharisees, and to some extent, the followers of John the Baptist, took pride in themselves and ceremonial fasting. Jesus's message however was not about ceremony but a transformed heart. They were holding on to the *old*. He offered the *new*. They were seeking the approval of *men*. He offered the approval of *God*. They practiced ritual, and sought righteousness through it. He offered a relationship with God and preached *grace*.

A few years after we had moved from Oregon to North Carolina, I flew into Portland, Oregon one night. As soon as I left the airport, I was pulled over by the police. I had not turned on the car's lights. The officer said, "I'll just need to check your license." He was gone for a long time. Finally, he came back and told me that my license was suspended. I told him that it must be a mistake. He told me it wasn't my NC license but my *Oregon* license that was suspended. But I had surrendered my Oregon license when I got my North Carolina license years before. That didn't matter, he told me, the state still suspended it! He gave me a ticket that cost five hundred dollars. I found out later that it was about our son's car. He had parked it at a Marine base when he was deployed to Afghanistan. The insurance had expired on it. Because my name was on the title and registration of the vehicle, the Oregon DMV had sent a notice to our old Oregon address, informing us that the vehicle insurance had lapsed, and they would suspend my license within thirty days if the insurance for the car was not paid. I had not lived in Oregon for five years, the DMV does not forward these notices. I had no way of knowing about the legal case that was developing and would soon bring so much trouble into my life. Our son was on the other side of the world and didn't know what was going on, either. I tried to explain all these circumstances to the police, to the Oregon DMV, and countless other people inside and outside of the DMV, but to no avail. The law was the law. When I returned to North Carolina, I decided to just pay the ticket. End of story, right? Wrong. Paying the fine was an admission of guilt. A few weeks later I got a notice from the *North Carolina* DMV informing me that because I had been "convicted" of driving with a suspended license in the state of Oregon, and because driving with a suspended license is such a very big no-no in North Carolina, they would were suspending my NC license. I could appeal their decision, get legal counsel, etc. A few days after that I got another notice. It was from my insurance company. They were notified by the state of NC that because I was pending suspension of driver's license, they would be cancelling my insurance because I was now considered high risk. I called my agent right away and explained the circumstances. He was sorry but there was nothing he could do. However, he consoled me, I could get insurance through Lloyds of London for about $1500 a month. He would be glad to send over their application.

After nearly a year of failed appeals, and in a last desperate act, I called the clerk of the Oregon court in which I had paid the fine. I told her what had happened and how it was ruining my life. You know what she did? She went into the chambers of the judge and spoke for me. She went in as my advocate. The judge listened to her and decided to vacate the judgment against me. The judge signed a court order. It was faxed from the courthouse in Oregon to North Carolina. I was cleared! What a relief it was when the kindness of that judge overturned the law against me.

Okay, that is a long story, but yours might be also. I mean that the law of God is a judgment against you that has been developing since the day you were born. It doesn't matter if you're unaware of your guilt or think you're not guilty. *You are*. It doesn't matter if you think God doesn't have jurisdiction over you. *He does*. Your only hope is to have Jesus Christ as your Advocate. Because of His holiness and His death on the cross for you, God listens to Him on your behalf so that the case against you can be dismissed (Heb.7:25). In Mark's gospel and in this text, Jesus steps in to defend the disciples on the basis of their relationship to Him. He presents Himself as a bridegroom, and the disciples as His attendants. You need this same kind of relationship. Do you want it? It can be yours. Right now just say to Him, "Lord Jesus, I'm unaware of everything, but I know I am guilty. Would You come into my life and be my Advocate before Almighty God?" He is ready to hear you and take up your case. Once you do this and are in this relationship with Him, stay in that relationship. Here is how:

Don't Let the "Serious" Get in the Way of Joy. In our text, the disciples are asked, "How is it that John's disciples and the disciples of the Pharisees are fasting but yours are not?" (Mark 2:18). The question is a criticism that comes from a legalistic, lost, and unredeemed heart. In their efforts to please God, the Pharisees had created a burdensome system of rules and regulations that were to be observed with the utmost seriousness. The Apostle Paul warns us against such systems and misdirected seriousness: "Do not go beyond what is written" (1Cor.4:6).

Just before all of this Jesus is at the home of Levi (Matthew), eating and drinking. Peter and Andrew and James and John are with Him at the home of His new disciple, a tax collector. The Pharisees and their followers had been watching all this, and they did not like seeing the disciples and the tax collectors – all these sinners – riding over the waves of the world with the Savior, while they struggled to stay afloat in their own scheming sea of self-righteousness. These were naturally gloomy people. The way of Jesus and His followers was distressing to their joyless lives. They were resentful. If we're not careful, we can become this way, too. If we trust in Jesus as the Son of God, we should be changed from a resentful observer to a joyous participant in His gracious ways with everyone. As the Apostle Paul says, "May the God of hope fill you with all joy and peace as you trust in Him" (Rom.15:13). All joy and peace in life comes from knowing Him who is the greatest joy of all. Unless we know Him, we can become clouded by misplaced seriousness and gloom about ourselves or others and fall into false judgment.

Don't Let the "Sacred" Get in the Way of Salvation. Jesus asks in verse 19, "How can the guests of the bridegroom fast while he is with them?" At the close of a wedding feast the bride's parents would escort her to the bridal chamber, and the bridegroom would then say farewell and go to his bride. "When I am taken away from them," Jesus implies, "then it would be right for them to mourn and fast." When Jesus is with them, why should they fast over Moses? Instead, they are so glad to be with Him.

In the Old Testament, the fast of the Day of Atonement was required (Lev.16:29,31; 23:27-32; Num.29:7). After the Exile, four other annual fasts were observed by the Jews (Zech.7:5; 8:19). Later on, the Pharisees added fasting twice a week on Monday and Tuesday (cf. Luke 18:12). According to these sacred traditions, Moses had gone up on Mt. Sinai on a Thursday and had come down on a Monday. So they were known to fast on these two days. That is why in Luke 18 the Pharisee declares, "I fast twice a week…"(Luke 18:12). Here in Mark 2:19 Jesus is saying, in effect, "I am more honorable than Moses. You might fast to mark his coming and going, but I am not gone. My disciples are like the friends of the bridegroom, and that is who I am. I have not left the party yet!" The disciples probably fasted when Jesus was taken from them and was crucified.

We should mourn when we have lost a sense of His presence or when our sins have disturbed our relationship with Him. When you know that you have grieved His Spirit, when you have lost a sense of His presence in your life, then you should fast and mourn and pray so that communion with Him is restored. But you must never, ever, forget the good news: the Bridegroom has made *you* His friend. The joy of this relationship with Him is yours. Don't be bullied by sacred notions about Moses or anyone else, but be discipled by the grace of God revealed to you in Jesus Christ.

Don't Let the Old Get in the Way of the New. Look at verses 21-22. Jesus explains, "No one sews a patch of unshrunk cloth on an old garment. If he does, the *new piece* will pull away from the old, making the tear worse. And no one pours *new wine* in old wineskins. If he does, the new wine will burst the skins and both the wine and the wineskins will be ruined. No, he pours new wine into new wineskins" (Mark 2:21-22).

Jesus's relationship to us and ours to Him is a "new piece of cloth" and "new wine." These phrases have powerful implications for our thinking and outlook because these are ways of describing the new covenant (Matt.26:28). The old covenant was all used up. It was the dusk of Moses and the dawn of Jesus Christ.

In the gospel of John, the story is told of how Jesus attended a wedding at Cana. Do you remember what he did for His mother and His friends? They needed wine, so He made new wine. And how was that new wine? It was superior to everything that the wedding guests had been drinking. The master of the feast called the bridegroom and said to Him,

> "Every man at the beginning sets out the good wine, and when the guests have well drunk, then the inferior. You have kept the good wine until now!" John 2:9-10

In the same way, for us as friends of the bridegroom, the very best has come. We can never be satisfied with the old again. The old covenant (along with the old ways of sin) no longer satisfies us. We've be relocated by God, moved from our old address, with its old patterns of dealing with conflict, anger, bitterness, rage and pride, to our new life, our new address in Christ. We have tasted the new wine, the very best wine, and nothing else is like it. As the Apostle Paul writes,

> For when we were controlled by the sinful nature, the sinful passions aroused by the law were at work in our bodies, so that we bore fruit for death. But now, by dying to what once bound us, we have been released from the law so that we serve in the new way of the Spirit and not in the old way of the written code. Rom.7:5

We live now in the new way of the Spirit. Every part of our life, everything that happens to us now, even our most severe trials, are under God's grace and working for our good (Rom. 8:28, James 1:2). If we turn to Him and trust in Him, our old condemned identity in Adam's race has expired at the cross and no longer has any bearing in our standing with God. We are now released from the law! Don't let misplaced seriousness, false judgement, sacred notions, or old traditions get in the way of the joy of your salvation and the new life you have in Christ Jesus. The old address is no more. We have a new ID with a new song (Rev.2:17, 5:9).

Don't let your past life, your current life, or any time in your life, get in the way of the new life you have or can have in Jesus Christ. When it comes to the law, you need this Advocate. The God of all heaven and earth is listening to Him! He is ready to overturn and vacate all the judgments against you, not because you're innocent. You are guilty but His Son has taken all the punishment of the law on the cross for you and now He lives forever to intercede on your behalf (Heb.7:25). This is the grace of God that can cleanse you, save you, renew you, and guide you for the rest of your life.

The Angry Lord of the Sabbath

Mark 3:1-6

> He looked around at them in anger and, deeply distressed at their stubborn hearts, said to the man, "Stretch out your hand," and his hand was completely restored. Mark 3:5

As one of the strongest storms in history came across the Carribean, the governor of Florida told people to flee. "We can rebuild your home," he said, "but we cannot rebuild your life." As I heard that comment, it struck me again that these terrible storms expose how powerless and defenseless I am in this world. How much we are in need of One who has overcome death and who holds the power to make life new, whether that is the revitalization people need after such a storm has smashed their homes or the resurrection of life after the physical death that we all will someday experience. We declare that name today. One of the churches involved in helping distribute emergency supplies to Floridians and directly located in the storm's path has this posted:

> God is our refuge and strength, always ready to help in times of trouble. Psalm 46:1

The healing of this man with the withered hand by Jesus in Mark 3:1-6 is the last in five conflicts recorded by Mark, culminating in the plot of Jesus's antagonists to kill Him. Rabbinical teaching allowed for the treating of the sick or injured on the Sabbath, *if* life was actually in danger, but if there was no risk of death, then treating someone was not permitted. Was it permissible for a disabled man to be in the synagogue? He could not have been admitted to the temple, but we are not sure about synagogue tradition. With all that has gone on previously it seems possible that this man was actually planted in the synagogue. They are out to get Jesus. Why is Jesus angry and what is it exactly that makes Him angry? How should the anger He displays influence our own lives?

We associate anger with sinfulness. Anyone can get angry. In the book of Psalms we are told to "flee from anger," but the Apostle Paul says, "Be angry and sin not" (Eph. 4:26). And we know that as the book of James says, "Everyone should be quick to listen slow to speak and slow to become angry for man's anger does not bring about the righteous life that God desires" (James 1:19-20).

As the Son of God, Jesus was angry but it was not sinful anger because the motive behind His anger was right. It was righteous anger.

What Makes Him Angry? Look at verses 1-2. You can find the answer right there: "Some of them were looking for a reason to accuse Him." They are watching to see if Jesus will heal him, and they want to accuse Him. They knew Jesus could heal people, but they were more concerned with getting rid of Jesus than for the welfare of the sick man. Here is Jesus, the "Lord of the Sabbath," as He called Himself, the One who holds all the blessings of creation and rest and forgiveness and healing. It was the hardness of hearts that angered Him- the purposeful and willful blindness that sins against the Holy Spirit. They were unwilling to open their ears, unwilling to see, unwilling to accept what they saw and heard, just as they were later on in Mark 3:22: **"**He is possessed by Beelzebub! By the prince of demons, He is driving out demons."

This is why the wrath of God comes upon people: it comes because they willfully subvert, ignore, and distort the truth about themselves and the truth about God. As the Apostle Paul summarizes,

> …the wrath of God is being revealed from heaven against all the godlessness and wickedness of men who suppress the truth by their wickedness. Rom.1:18

After the Columbia space shuttle disintegrated during its return to Earth, a series of tests were conducted in San Antonio, Texas. The purpose was to establish the actual cause of the disaster that claimed the lives of seven astronauts. People investigating the accident agreed that the cause was a loose piece of foam insulation that was dislodged during the launch. It slammed into the wing of the spacecraft with enough mass and force to create a hole. During reentry, superheated air entered through this hole and thus began the disintegration of Columbia. The mission was doomed at the outset. The evidence was so persuasive that there remained no reasonable doubt among the investigators about the physical cause of the accident. But a series of tests had already been planned to reenact the accident. A piece of foam was to be fired at the wing panels. NASA officials approached the investigation team and asked them to cancel the tests because they would have to use the only remaining spare space shuttle wing panel in existence. The cost of the panel? $700,000. Afterall, NASA officials argued, why go through with the simulation if the evidence was conclusive? But one engineer on the investigation board realized that despite the overwhelming evidence, many people at NASA still stubbornly believed that a piece of foam could not have caused Columbia's destruction. He argued that if the culture of the agency was ever going to change at NASA, these people would have to be confronted with the most tangible proof possible.

What does it take for *us* to realize what is true? What does it take to break down the defiance and resistance that aids us so naturally when we are in the wrong? It is this kind of hardness of heart that angers Jesus. It is this culture of unbelief that He seeks to change.

Is Jesus's anger really justified? Look at verses 3-4. It says, "But they remained silent." They had no answer. We have no answer. Their silence was not the silence of respect or deference, but the silence of those who have the truth right in front of them but refuse to give in. They refuse to acknowledge the Lord of eternal life before them. If they answer Jesus they will expose their hostility and be seen for who they are. It is also the silence of those who refuse to answer honestly; the silence of rebels who have chosen to take up war against the gracious Savior God. In our own time, the silence is because we are stubborn and stuck in sin, and holding on to the fiction that God doesn't exist, and that there is no such thing as truth. Just like these accusers, we have spent all our ammunition and have no real defense. It is exactly as the Apostle Paul says,

> Now we know that whatever the law says it says to those under the law so that every mouth may be silenced and the whole world held accountable to God. Romans 3:19

Jesus's anger was justified not simply because these people were sinful and spiritually withered with dead hearts, but because they were not in the synagogue that day to listen to God. They were not there to learn. They were not there to hear the message that would save them and renew them. They were not there to worship Him. They had come for other reasons. They wanted to trouble Him and trap Him. They didn't want to hear a word from Him. How different they are than Cornelius in the Book of Acts who asks Peter to come to his house so that he can hear the word of the Lord. Cornelius says, "Now we are all here in the presence of God to listen to everything the Lord has commanded you to tell us" (Acts 10:33). What a sobering thought; that gatherings and places could be like this.

There is more to life and all these places than meets the eye. This is more than just a sermon I've been working on. There is more. O God, may there be more! May what you hear today be "everything that Lord has commanded" me to tell you. And this place, and every place of worship, every place we gather, the sanctuaries, the rooms in the lower level, the second floor, the third floor, our homes, the lunchroom table where Bible studies are happening, the place where you are right now - all of it -could be thought of this way: *We are all here in the presence of God!*

What accompanies Jesus's anger? Look at verses 4-5. They were not at the synagogue to worship, but to conspire, to accuse, to advance their own kingdom not the kingdom of God. Jesus's anger is justified, but notice what accompanies His anger. It says, "He looked around at them in anger, and *deeply distressed* at their stubborn hearts" (NIV) or "grieved at the hardness of their hearts" (KJV). You and I often delight and rejoice in evil, but God *grieves* over it.

> The Lord saw how great man's wickedness on earth had become and that every inclination of the thoughts of his heart was only evil all the time. The Lord was grieved that He had made man on the earth and His heart was filled with pain. Gen.6:5-6

It is the grief of God's love that accompanies the anger of Jesus. We who have broken the law of God must finally face the love of God. His wrath is really the wrath of His love. What is said by those condemned in Revelation 6:16?

> They called to the mountains and the rocks, "Fall on us and hide us from the face of Him who sits on the throne and from <u>the wrath of the Lamb</u>.

The wrath of the sacrificial Lamb is really the wrath of love. Love spurned provokes God's anger. We who have broken the law of God *must face the love of God.*

The tests in San Antonio for NASA were conducted using a compressed 35 foot rectangular barrel, nitrogen-pressurized gun that is normally used to fire dead chickens against aircraft surfaces to test structural integrity against bird strikes. They fired the gun several times over a period of several days at different velocities and angles attempting to recreate what had happened on the launch pad. Some of the NASA engineers remained defiant, belittling the slight damage caused, thinking they were vindicated. On the last day of the experiment, and with help from the recovered flight data recorder of the Columbia, the investigators finally had the exact information they needed to simulate what had happened. They were able to duplicate the trajectory, angle, and velocity of what happened at launch. Among the NASA engineers watching were many who were still in denial. The gun was fired and sent a suitcase-sized piece of foam hurtling into the wing panel at 800 kilometers (500 miles) per hour. The blast was so strong that it broke one of the gauges tracking the experiment. When the smoke cleared there was an audible gasp from the crowd. The hole created in the wing panel was 16 inches across, big enough to put your head through. Some in the crowd began to cry. They realized now that it was all true.

Perhaps you're listening to this sermon, and you do not believe. You think, "I'm fine. I'm as good as anybody and better than most people." But what the Scriptures teach and what you don't realize is that you're badly, mortally damaged. You are damaged and in danger of perishing. How many "shots" from the cannon of experience does it take before you to believe it? How many holes must be blown in your heart? We have so many excuses, so many reasons, for our behavior and attitudes. We are so resistant to the truth about ourselves: we are sinners, born sinners, like David says, "Surely I was sinful at birth, sinful from the time my mother conceived me" (Ps. 51:5).

Unless God intevenes in our lives and awakens us, unless the smoke clears from our minds, and we finally see, we're doomed. You were damaged at launch, and when the time comes to return to God, the truth will be revealed. God brought you here today so that you could investigate these things, and by His grace, see the truth. Don't be defiant. Turn to Him now, before you return to the earth.

Warning to the World

Mark 3:20-35

> But whoever blasphemes against the Holy Spirit will never be forgiven. He is guilty of an eternal sin. Mark 3:29

The "golden hour" in major trauma centers is the one hour window following an accident in which someone's injuries can successfully treated so that they can recover and live. The gospel is the "golden hour" for the wounds of humanity's sins. Now is the day of salvation in Mark's Gospel.

Chapter 3 is a very sad chapter in Mark's gospel. Jesus is rejected by both the political and spiritual leadership of Israel as it tells us in Mark 3:6, "Then then Pharisees went out and began to plot with the Herodians how they might kill Jesus." He is rejected and then it gets worse! These same leaders imply that Jesus is using the power of the devil. How should we interpret these verses?

Bad News for Satan

> The teachers of the law who came down from Jerusalem said, "He is possessed by Beelzebub. By the prince of demons He is driving out demons." Mark 3:22

Beelzebub translated is "Lord of "zebub" or "flies." Flies were associated with sickness and disease, so the name of the god was interpreted as 'Lord of the flies'; a god who could cause or cure diseases.

In our text the crowds are coming from every direction. Just touching Him brings healing. People are coming from everywhere we are told in Mark 3:7-8. They are coming from Galilee. They are coming from Judea. They are coming from as far away as Jerusalem, as far away as Idumea, even beyond the Jordan to the east (Perea), even from far north, Tyre and Sidon (Syria). Why are they coming?? It is the *golden hour*. He is curing them! He is healing them! Casting out evil spirits! People are bringing their family, bringing their sick friends. The lame are walking! The blind are seeing! The deaf can hear! The sick are healthy again! The cancer is gone! The disease is gone! The greatest display of the power of God. But what do these "teachers of the law" say?! "This is power of the devil." So this is a very sad chapter. Jesus responds in verses 23-27. It says, "Jesus called them." And He asks them, "How can Satan cast out Satan?" He delivers some bad news to Satan and refutes them with three simple examples:

First, a kingdom. How can a kingdom divided stand? It cannot, it dissolves into civil war.

Second, a home. How can a divided house keep it together? It cannot, it dissolves into separation and divorce.

Third, hell itself. In effect, Jesus says, "Your idea of Satan driving out Satan is just as impossible as these examples I've given." Satan is a great, real, and personal power directing war against God and those who look to Him in faith. He is not going to oppose himself! He is like a strong man and this world is his house. He has to be overpowered and tied up by someone even stronger who can then "carry off his possessions."

What Jesus has shown in all of the healings and driving out of demons is that someone stronger than Satan has gotten into his house. Through a window left open, Jesus Christ has gone around the usual security systems upon which the realm of the devil depends. What I mean is that our own human and ordinary conception and birth guarantees our sin and weakness and inability to stand up to the devil. But *Jesus divinely bypassed ordinary conception and birth*. He has come as a human being, but He is born of a virgin and untouched by sin. In Mark 1:12-13 Satan tries to ruin Him in the wilderness, but He is without sin and too strong! Jesus has slipped into Satan's realm through the window of the virgin Mary's womb. Throughout Mark's gospel, He meets up with the house guards, Satan's demons, and tells them, "Be quiet and do exactly as I say." And they obey. This is very bad news for Satan. But such good news for us!

Good News for the Weary

> "I tell you the truth all the sins and blasphemies of men will be forgiven them." Mark 3:28

Through the power of His forgiveness, all of my sins and all of my blasphemies, no matter what they are or what I've done, no matter what I've said, no matter how massive the chains are, I've got a *new life* through the forgivness of my sins.

As I said, Chapter 3 is a sad chapter. The political and religious establishment of Israel wants Jesus dead. They want to stop Him, discredit Him, and kill Him so that all He is doing will stop. How sad for the Jewish leaders to do this! It is the demise of Israel. But look at the most important thing Jesus has done in Chapter 3 just before. The leadership of the twelve tribes is rejecting Him, but in

Mark 3:13-19, the Twelve Apostles are appointed. Jesus is replacing the leadership of Israel. He is forming a new Israel. His message of grace and forgiveness is going out to ALL THE EARTH waiting to receive Him through the message of the Apostles.

A new kind of nation, a new kind of family, based not on the flesh but on the message of the Apostles, on following Him, and doing His will. Relationships will now be based on Him and on doing the will of God. Even Jesus's own family, who think He's gone off His rocker, has to learn about a new kind of family, not based on flesh but on the proclamation about Jesus that the Twelve will make to all the world. This is the good news for the world. Jesus also gives the world a warning.

Warning to the World

> "But whoever blasphemes against the Holy Spirit will never be forgiven, but is guilty of an eternal sin." Mark 3:29

How should we understand this difficult verse? It is a warning to people who do not believe to be very careful of their words and thoughts about God and Jesus. This is a sin that is much more common than you might think, and there may be many who have committed it. Over years of pastoral ministry, I've talked to Christians who have worried that they had done or said something that constitutes the unforgiveable sin. But here Jesus is not addressing believers. He is not talking about what they might do or say or think. He is addressing those who do not believe. He is addressing an obstinate pattern of thinking towards the light of God's revelation of Himself and His grace in Jesus Christ. If we use these "teachers of the law" as an example, the unforgiveable sin is the culmination of their headstrong, willful, unyielding, inflexible, unbending, intransigent, and intractable attitude toward God's revelation of Himself in Jesus. Such obstinance is noticeable and widespread today, and it may be very close to the unforgiveable sin.

The teachers of the law were seeing all that Jesus was doing, but they were distorting and twisting it, and denying who He was and denying the power of God. Their state of mind toward Him had been shaped over a period of time after they had heard about Him. It began in an embryonic state of doubt or skepticism, but it matured into blasphemy. Sadly, it seems that they were now guilty of this "eternal sin," and none of them would be saved. On the other hand, there were others like Nicodemus and some of the other Pharisees, who, as they learned about Jesus, first doubted but then came to believe in Him.

This verse warns us to be more aware of thoughts and judgments about Jesus. He warns people who read the Bible but who persist in calling it rubbish. He warns those who are skeptical. He warns those who say, "Jesus, was a good man, a great teacher, but nothing more." He warns those who say, "There is no God and we certainly don't need forgiveness from God. There is no such thing as sin! These Christians who say these things are only describing a psychological thing in their own heads, and nothing more than that." Jesus warns those who look at Earth and all of creation declaring God's existence and glory but who dismiss it all as "mere evolution." He warns those who say, "There was no 'creator' or 'creation'. Earth is just a lucky damp rock, and we're surrounded by the leftovers of a big explosion in the cosmos." If you persist in thinking such things and saying such things as this, *then you are in danger*. You may not be far from an unforgiveable sin.

God does not want you to perish. If you are worried that you're guilty of committing such a sin, go back to verse 28: "I tell you the truth, All the sins and blasphemies of men will be forgiven them." It is the golden hour still. Always look at verse 28 before verse 29. Everything can and will be forgiven *if* you receive and trust Him. Satan cannot stop Him from forgiving you or keep you from following Him. We will sin in thought, word, and deed, but if instead of despairing and giving up, we look to our Savior's mercy to restore us, God will continue to plunder the devil's house. Even when we morally fail, even when we sin, we remain His. Every time we give ourselves to His work, when you have the opportunity to forgive someone; when you help someone or call someone or greet someone with patience and kindness in this busy and rushed world, God takes a little more away from the devil. When it comes to your life, Almighty God wants to clean the devil out and leave him with nothing.

Jesus Christ came into the realm of the devil in order to free you from the weariness of sin and bondage and to carry you away for Himself. He came to take away from Satan what Satan thought he had secured for himself. When we trust in Christ, when we turn to Him, God is robbing the devil of every pleasure and every satisfaction that was his when you lived under his power and will. Under the power of sin you were lying, lusting, cheating, stealing, gossiping, scheming, and threatening, but then Jesus broke into the devil's realm. He went to the cross to stretch out those arms for you, and the devil could not stop Him from loving you and dying for you. If you do not know Him, if you are trapped in the devil's house, look to Jesus and believe in Him. The strong arms of God are ready to carry you to safety.

The Repentance We Need

Mark 6:1-2,7,12,20

> They went out and preached that people should repent.
> Mark 6:12

I have chosen these readings from Mark 6 to summarize and emphasize three points about repentance. What is important to all Christians is belief in Jesus Christ as the Son of God who alone saves us from our sins. Through His wisdom and grace, He draws us to Himself, awakening us, forgiving us, changing and turning our hearts, giving us new life in Himself. It is all summed up in the message of the disciples as given in our text. Repentance is the principal and ongoing work and effect of the gospel in our lives.

Although the culture we live in is very different and far removed from this ancient culture in which the disciples spoke, we are still committed to the gospel message. We ought to spend our energy getting this message out instead of struggling over disagreements about it. The problem of human sin is so great a burden! In order to be brought into a restored relationship with God and one another, through God's grace human beings must be turned away from sin, must be repulsed by their sin, must indeed, *hate* their sin. As an old Anglican confession asks: *Do you abhor your sins from the bottom of your heart?* How exactly does one have this "bottom of your heart" experience of repentance? Consider these passages and three things that are present in message of the gospel.

Wisdom

First of all, in the preaching of the gospel and the call to repentance there is always *wisdom* that makes me want to change my life. It says in our text, "Jesus left there and went to His hometown, accompanied by His disciples. When the Sabbath came, He began to teach in the synagogue, and many who heard Him were amazed. "Where did He get these things?" they asked. "What's this wisdom that has been given to Him, that He even does miracles?" (Mark 6:2).

When Jesus spoke, it was so amazing! His words evoked and stirred people. It doesn't tell us what He said here but we know that He really made people think and reflect. He made their minds work like they had never worked before. The preaching of the gospel should always be like this- it seems foolish to the world but in fact it is filled with wisdom that stimulates our minds and causes us to think and consider our lives. The gospel causes us to ponder and explore what we think, what we believe and how we live.

As the Apostle Paul writes, "We preach Christ crucified: a stumbling block to Jews and foolishness to Gentiles, but to those who are called both Jews and Greeks, Christ the power of God and the wisdom of God" (1Cor. 1:24). We hear this message and we start to struggle and want to make changes. We want to do something.

Through the work of the Holy Spirit, wisdom starts to unfold in us. It is like this little tiny ball-like object that my wife carries around in her purse. I looks like a ball but at the grocery store she takes it out, and starts unfolding it. It becomes a bag. It holds everything she buys. This is what happens in our minds when we hear experience the gospel. It unfolds to hold everything. We begin to unfold its wisdom. In Colossians 2:3 the Apostle Paul says that in Christ "are hidden all the treasures of wisdom." The gospel of Jesus unfolds to encompass and hold so much more than we ever imagined.

Jesus Christ commands us in effect, "Unfold Me! Discover that every treasure, everything valuable, is found in Me. Find out that every concern of your life is contained in Me." When people encounter the living Jesus Christ in the preaching of the gospel, when they are stirred by the message about Him, turn to Him and repent, they are experiencing unfolding wisdom! As Paul says in 1 Corinthians 1:30, "Christ Jesus … has become for us wisdom from God."

Power

Along with wisdom there is also in the preaching of repentance, *power* that changes our life. "Calling the Twelve to Him, He sent them out two by two and gave them authority over evil spirits. … They went out and preached that people should repent. They drove out many demons and anointed many sick people with oil and healed them" (Mark 6:6,12,13).

The proclamation has the power to change human nature. Think about it carefully. What did the miracles of Jesus actually signify or represent? The miracles of Jesus most importantly and supremely signify Jesus's power to grant the forgiveness of our sins and to give us new life. Above all, forgiveness is a mighty power. The miracles of Jesus, the powerful things that He did were meant to show the power He had to forgive our sins. What does He tell the teachers of the law when He heals the paralyzed man in Mark 2:10? "That you may know that the Son of Man has authority on earth to forgive sins… I tell you, get up, take up your mat and walk."

The man is instantly and fully restored. The miraculous healing was the sign that his sins were forgiven entirely and completely at that very moment. For us today the sign of forgiveness that we are granted is the presence and power of the Holy Spirit working in our lives. Paul says in Ephesians 1:13, "Having believed you were marked in Him with a seal, the promised Holy Spirit." In the miracles, the healings, the driving out of demons done by Jesus and the disciples He sent out, and in the repentance of people who received their message, we are seeing the mighty power of forgiveness. A heart *can* be made new. Wounds *can* be healed. But this was not just for them, now we also can experience the forgiveness of sins, and be turned away from sin, and by the work of the Holy Spirit can have the power to get up from whatever is paralyzing us. You can, should, and will walk away from whatever has diminished you, from whatever is tempting you, from whatever has enslaved you. How will people overcome the problem of the heart that has reduced all of humanity to the conniving, sex trafficking, slave-making, school shooting people that our world has become? The power of the forgiveness of our sins by Jesus Christ. The forgiveness of Jesus gives people the power to walk in new life, the power to go out, the power to overcome, to no longer be under the dominion of sin, but to live in

Character

Finally, in the preaching of the gospel and the call to repentance, there must and will be a change in our character. Those who proclaim the message must themselves be changed by it. "Herod feared John and protected him, knowing him to be a righteous and holy man" (Mark 6:20). Even someone as godless and lost and wicked as Herod could tell that John the Baptist was someone who really believed in the truth. He knew that he was listening to someone who actually practiced what he believed and talked about. When we listen to someone we want to know, do they really believe this? With John, you had no doubt. Herod knew who John was. He knew how he lived and conducted himself and Herod noticed, "Here is someone very different from me."

Think of the relationship that Billy Graham had with some of our presidents and you get a picture of this. The modern Herods of our times have all known Billy Graham. The have all known that he really believed the message of the cross and that he had been changed by it himself. In a very Herod-like way, they have all enjoyed listening to him. Graham was an unusual man, a changed man, changed by the wisdom and the power of the gospel. In the same way there was no doubt when people listened to the Apostle Paul and, by God's grace and mighty power, there will be no doubt when people know us and listen to us.

Paul spells out, in detail, the remarkable change in character this way: "Do you not know that the wicked will not inherit the kingdom of God? Do not be deceived; Neither the sexually immoral, nor idolaters, nor adulterers, nor male prostitutes, nor homosexual offenders, nor thieves, nor the greedy, nor drunkards, nor slanderers, nor swindlers will inherit the kingdom of God. And that is what some of you were. But you were washed, you were sanctified, you were justified in the name of the Lord Jesus Christ and by the Spirit of God" (1Cor.6:9-11).

He doesn't mention every kind of change, but these are a few powerful examples of repentance of what happens when we turn to Christ; when He knocks at the door of our lives and we answer. And we could go on with examples. The gospel changes us from impatient to patient, from wrathful to loving, from critical to encouraging, from anxious to peaceable, from silly to serious, from emptiness to fullness, from hard-hearted to kind-hearted, from pompous to humble, from complainers to companions. These examples and thousands upon thousands and ten thousands upon ten thousands more will come forth wherever this gospel unfolds.

Let's spend ourselves this way: unfolding the message of grace in our own lives, sharing it, living it, proclaiming it, and putting our whole life into it. Everything can fit there! This message, and no other, contains the wisdom and power that changes us all the way down to the bottom of our hearts.

The Leader We Need

Mark 6:30-44

Do you know about the prayer of Moses when Joshua is about to be appointed to succeed him?

> May the Lord, the God of the spirits of all mankind appoint a man over this community to go out and come in before them, one who will lead them out and bring them in so that the Lord's people will not be like sheep without a shepherd. Numbers 27:15-17

That was Moses's prayer for people, and in Israel's history, Joshua was the immediate fulfillment. But this language is pointing beyond Joshua. It is pointing to only One Person - a man of such remarkable compassion and courage, One Man appointed by God, a man willing and empowered to enter into the full and complete darkness of humanity as the True Shepherd, the Good Shepherd, going after people to lead them out of their helplessness and danger and bring them in where they would be safe. In these verses we are learning about Jesus. What kind of leader is Jesus? One who understands our limits, who has compassion, and One who plans on *using* us.

How to Build a Fire

> The apostles gathered round Jesus and reported to Him all they done and taught. Then because so many people were coming and going that they did not even have a chance to eat, he said to them, "Come with me by

yourselves to a quiet place and get some rest." Mark 6:30-31

The apostles are reporting back to Him the details of their deeds and words, and He looks at them and sees that they are tired and weary. Those who are involved in ministry will know this: It can be very tiring. There is just so much "coming and going." And this is where the biblical concept of a retreat is found. It is not more conferences and classes, not more coming and going– it is rest.

Jesus is showing us how to build a fire. You don't build a fire by piling and stacking wood tightly. You have to pay careful attention to the space you are leaving between the pieces of wood. That is how the fire is able to burn. The breathing space between the pieces is just as important as the wood. Jesus says to them, "Come with Me by yourselves …get some rest." Nowadays, He might add, "And everyone give Me your cellphones."

That is the kind of leadership we need; that thinks about the quiet places, the quiet spaces between all the activity. We need to know that His eyes are on us, too, caring for us, and that He wants us to have time in our lives where there no more planning, no more texting, no more emailing, Facebook, or WeChat. In the home, in the life of the church, Jesus knows when we cannot go on. As a leader under The Leader, I need to remember that He cares.

Do we know how to build a fire? When I have a meeting in the church or you lead a meeting and it starts at 7:30, and should be over by 10, but is dragging on until 11:00, 11:30 or even midnight; are we aware of people's limits?! This might be a problem in our church and many congregations. Our meetings go so long, even though so much nowadays could be done differently to help streamline things. Are we building a fire or quenching the flames of service? Are we a little like King Saul? He commanded the army not to eat until they had completely defeated the Philistines.

> Now the men of Israel were in distress that day, because Saul had bound the people under an oath, saying, 'Cursed by any man who eats food before evening comes, before I have avenged myself on my enemies!' So none of the troops tasted food. 1Samuel 14:24

Saul wanted to get his enemies. He pushed his people too hard and wouldn't allow them to even eat. Jesus knows how to build a fire and is saying, in effect, "That is enough. It's 10:00, let's stop. No more battling the enemy and evil, no more ministry meeting, no more board meeting, no more prayer meeting, no more nothing, no more coming and going." He knows our limits and wants us to have rest and restoration!

His Compassion on Us

> When Jesus landed and saw a large crowd, He had compassion on them, because they were like sheep without a shepherd. So He began teaching them many things. Mark 6:34

Jesus, we are told, began to teach them many things. We either need to receive ministry or we're being called to give ministry. The large crowd had no knowledge of God. They needed to receive ministry. They were lost, helpless, bewildered, and full of pain. When Jesus spoke, the very authority of God was felt by the people listening. Unlike other teachers, He didn't speak about God, He spoke for God. The singular and striking attention and the attachment of the crowds to Him and their amazement at His teaching underscores His unique authority and exclusive claims as the Son of God.

In Franklin Graham's eulogy at his father's funeral, he was very intentional about explaining his father's belief in the Bible. Billy Graham held to an unwavering position on the exclusive claims of Jesus about Himself as the only begotten Son of God and the only way to God. A highly regarded historian from American University, and who also happens to be Jewish, commented that he appreciated much of what Franklin Graham had said about his father, but he thought it was regrettable and unfortunate that Franklin had used the occasion of his father's funeral to promote his own narrow evangelical views.

Franklin Graham, however, was correct about Christianity and his father's belief. The truth is that if you do not believe in Jesus, you are a sheep without a shepherd. You are no more safe than a dumb animal in the blackest and most dreadful storm, for which no one cares or has any compassion. But if you know Him, (and you can), if you believe in Him (and you should) there is no better place, no safer place, than under His leadership. He cares about you.

His Plans for Us

> By this time it was late in the day, so His disciples came to Him. "This is a remote place," they said, "and it's already late. Send the people away …" But He answered, "You give them something to eat." Mark 6:35-37

Jesus uses the crowd's physical hunger to show that this ministry of caring, leading, and feeding His people must continue through the disciples, through us. We are called into ministry. Jesus tells them, "*You* give them something to eat" (Mark 6:37). He is asking something that is impossible, a task way beyond their powers. Some say that Jesus's only miracle here was that He encouraged greater sharing among the people, but that comes from a skepticism that dismisses what the text says. Verse 41 tells us exactly how much food they had to start with - 5 loaves and 2 fish.

The text is not talking about sharing but about the miracle of so many being fed with so little. This is exactly what our Leader is doing *through us*. He does not want the crowd simply focused on His miraculous power but on His ministry *through the disciples* so He tells them have all the people sit down in groups (Mark 6:39).

The multitude does not see what happens. Jesus takes the little food they have and blesses it. He performs the miracle, but gives the loaves and the fish to the disciples to distribute (Mark 6:41). From the perspective of everyone present - from all they could see - it was the disciples who were feeding them. Afterwards, the Twelve collect what is left over.

For our congregation, and in our lives, it should be no different. It doesn't matter if someone is moving or leaving. We have a task, a purpose in all our ministries and gatherings. "You give them something to eat," Jesus tells us. He wants to show Himself through us and every ministry of the church. It is a miracle ministry. We are under great stress, difficult conditions. How many crises do you have on any given weekday or on any given Sunday? In Christ you have a Leader who not only has compassion on you but is able to make Himself known *through you*.

Conditions are probably difficult in your life, but Jesus says "You give them something to eat!" When you sit down with a friend to listen to their troubles and share with them the truth that God has shown to you or how He has helped you or changed you, He will multiply it. He will work His miracle again and again when there is faith in Him.

If we trust in Him, then we must realize that we have a Leader whose intention is not that we should feel adequate for the task. His plan is not that we accept those tasks that seem equal to our powers, but rather that we should feel ourselves completely inadequate. That is the preparation and mindset we need, and that makes us ready to depend upon Him. Only in Him are we able to carry out His work, not just carrying on regardless of the conditions, but recognizing that these conditions are precisely where our Savior will display His power and make Himself known.

The Heart We Need

Mark 6:45-57, 7:1-30

The troubled human heart along with its care and treatment is a main theme of the Bible. Consider these passages:

> The Lord saw how great man's wickedness on the earth had become, and that every inclination of the thoughts of his heart was only evil all the time. Genesis 6:5

> The heart is deceitful above all things and beyond cure. Who can understand it? Jeremiah 17:9

> Above all else, guard your heart, for it is the wellspring of life. Proverbs 4:23

> If anyone is thirsty let him come to Me and drink. Whoever believes in Me, as the Scripture has said, streams of living water water will flow from within him. John 7:37

The Disciples Need Help

> For they had not understood about the loaves, their hearts were hardened. Mark 6:52

Maybe the disciples here, in the early part of their lives, are more like what we think of as "seekers." They had seen what took place when all the people were fed, but they didn't understand that what they had witnessed pointed to the true nature of Jesus as the Son of God. He will have to bring them back to these events, repeat things several times, and make them think through it all again (Mark 8:14-21). They will come to acknowledge who He is (Mark 8:27-30), but here it must be kept in mind that their spiritual condition may be more seeker-like. It is not final and complete, but initial and preparatory.

After the resurrection, an obvious transformation takes place in their understanding through the power of the Holy Spirit, just as they had been told, "...you will receive power when the Holy Spirit comes on you; and you will be my witnesses" (Acts 1:8). But even now, before the coming of the Holy Spirit, Jesus wants them to see Him for who He really is. He comes to them in their distress and exhaustion, and He looks like a ghost to them. They are tired. They are confused. They are frightened. He just seems to "pass them by."

Jesus wants their hearts to be transformed even now and to know that He is the One who shares in the name, nature, holiness, authority, power, majesty of the one true God who gloriously passed by Moses. God passed in front of Mosesbproclaiming, "The Lord, the Lord, the compassionate and gracious God, slow to anger, abounding in love and faithfulness, maintaining love to thousands and forgiving wickedness, rebellion, and sin" (Exodus 34:6-7).

Just as God spoke to Moses in the burning bush in the wilderness of Sinai, "I am who I am" (Exodus 3:14), Jesus tells His frightened friends, "Take courage, it is I. Don't be afraid." Like them, you, too, may have a hardened heart. You've seen and witnessed a lot. Maybe you kind of go along with the whole family and church thing. You identify as a Christian, but have no real interest in reading the Bible to understand it, in praying or in serving. Maybe the work of real repentance and turning your life over to Jesus has never happened. You need His help.

The Religious Leaders Need Help

> Isaiah was right when he prophesied about you hypocrites; as it is written: "These people honor me with their lips but their hearts are far from Me. They worship Me in vain: their teachings are but rules taught by men." You let go of the commands of God and are holding on to the traditions of men." And He said to them, "You have a fine way of setting aside the commands of God in order to observe your own traditions. Mark 7:6-9

Jesus tells these leaders that their problem is even more serious. These are the educated elite. They were the ones who were part of the great cultural conversation of their time. The tradition of the elders was a body of commentary and reflection of Israel's best teachers. A Pharisee was someone who was a recipient of this teaching. There was no commandment that required the Jews to wash, but we do find a mandate that the *priests* had to wash their hands and feet prior to entering the Tabernacle (Ex.30:19-21, c.f. 40.13). But in 2nd century BC, the *Pharisees assumed the purity laws of the priests* and began to wash their hands before morning prayer and pray: "Blessed be Thou O Lord King of the universe, who sanctified us by thy laws and commanded us to wash the hands."

For the Pharisees, all food was to be eaten as priestly food. Afterall, they reasoned, isn't all of Israel, a kingdom of *priests* according to Exodus 19:6? Eventually, the priestly regulations became obligatory for everyone. The intention of this might seem honorable enough: a desire to sanctify the ordinary acts of life and to demonstrate that Israel was devoted to God, but Jesus saw something else here and sharply condemned them.

They had missed the point. With all of their concern over piety they were reinforcing the delusion that sin can be dealt with in such superficial ways, ways that were unable to cleanse the *defilement of the heart*. The Pharisees and teachers of the law had elevated their own good intentions in order "to observe your own traditions." Worship is only true if it is based on the truth. With all their knowledge and understanding, they could not accept that their hearts were wrong. Jesus warns,

> Listen to me, everyone, and understand this. Nothing outside a man can make him unclean by going into him. Rather, it is what comes out of a man that makes him unclean. Mark 7:14-16

And consider what He says a few verses down:

> What comes out of a man is what makes him 'unclean.' For from within, out of men's hearts, come evil thoughts, sexual immorality, theft, murder, adultery, greed, malice, deceit, lewdness, envy, slander, arrogance and folly. All these evils come from inside and make a man unclean. Mark 7:20-23

Worship and all of life is only true if it is based upon truth revealed in Holy Scripture. I'm not going to get true life by what goes into me or because of whatever special diet I am on. Spiritual vitality does not come that way. In the same way, the "lips" can be deceptive. Whatever is said, whatever is sung, no matter how spiritual something looks, bears careful examination. Whether is it Islamic zeal, Jewish zeal, Buddhist zeal, Roman Catholic zeal or Presbyterian zeal.

You cannot tell what is acceptable to God by how great the church praise band is or by how great the praying is or by how much you feel like you're "being fed" or by the smiles. Not even "joy in the congregation" is the test of truth. According to Jesus, there is no real value to any kind of religious zeal. Worship is only true, it is only right, it is only good if it is based on what God has given us in His Word. The soundness of worship is not determined by what people are *singing* in church but by what they are *hearing* in church.

We Need Help (The Heart We Need)

> A woman whose little daughter was possessed by an evil spirit came and fell at His feet. The woman was a Greek, born in Syrian Phoenicia. She begged Jesus to drive the demon out of her daughter. "First let the children eat all they want, He told her, "for it is not right to take the children's bread and toss it to the dogs." "Yes, Lord," she replied, "but even the dogs under the table eat the children's crumbs." Mark 7:25-28

The Syrophoenician woman shows us the heart we need. (c.f. Luke 4:24-27). To this woman, Jesus was the only real hope for her circumstances. Yet as she comes to him begging, He refuses her. When He finally listens to her, He insults her, comparing her to an annoying dog. But she turns this insult into an insight. She accepts what Jesus tells her about herself. She doesn't try to get around it. She agrees with Him.

Notice that she calls Jesus "Lord." This is the only place in Mark's gospel where anyone calls Jesus "Lord." She gets it right, doesn't she? This One before whom she bowed down was the Lord of heaven and earth. Do I, do we, get it right? Am I, are we, ready to hear Him when He insults us? When the Bible calls us sinners, when the Bible calls us wicked, lost, and foolish? Martin Luther comments on this verse.

> Like her you must give God right in all He says against you and yet must not stand off from praying till you overcome as she overcame, till you have turned the very charges made against you into arguments and proofs of your need, till you too have taken Christ in His own words.

Luther knew the heart he needed and the heart we all need. This woman in our text shows us the kind of heart we need and the kind of heart we can have when we go to Jesus for His help. Isn't that why we are here today? This gathering is God's house, His "table," and all of us are here looking for food. Perhaps, you have been discouraged. We can sometimes be annoying to one another, all of us here crowded under His table. Perhaps, you have gone to Him crying out in need for help in the battle of life, trying to find some way to cope with the confidence-killing daily assault of petty degradations. Perhaps, as the Syrophoenician woman, you cried out for your child to be set free and He seems unconcerned. But yet we are here, here you are, under His table.

There is perhaps no creature more hopeful on all the earth than a dog waiting near a table. We have this dogged hope and trust that the Lord and Master of our life will feed us. We know He has food, don't we? If you have trusted Him as the Son of God who died for your sins, you know He has food, and there is no way He can chase you off. This is faith that never gives up even when it is put off or put down. Once upon a time, you were a stray dog, and He fed you. You will never leave Him alone. When you have the heart of a dog who has been fed, no one can chase you away from Him. You know that He hears those who cry to Him in their hour of need. You know that all praise and glory belongs to Him. That is the heart we need.

Years back I had surgery on my knee. While I was waiting for the surgery, a nurse came in and read carefully through the notes she had. She took out a red magic marker to mark my left knee as the one where surgery was to be performed. In big letters she wrote, "YES!" That is what we ought to be doing today. If we are those who truly seek the Lord, in a way we are writing "YES" over our *hearts*. We are in agreement with God's assessment of our condition. We are in agreement with the Great Physician and recognize that we need for Him to operate *here*. To heal us here. *Here, Lord,* we say, *start here, start now.*

The Understanding We Need

Mark 8:1-30

> "But what about you?" He asked, Who do you say that I am?" Mark 8:29

G. Campbell Morgan said of this passage that "Jesus made human opinion concerning Himself the supreme thing in His ministry." It isn't that human opinion can actually effect who Jesus is, nor that Jesus acted in such a way to please human opinion, but Jesus sought to *expose* what people thought of Him. Wherever His name is mentioned and whenever His name comes up, human opinion surfaces quickly.

Who Do Men Say I Am ?

Jesus asks this question, our text says, *on the road* or *along the way*. Jesus and the disciples are traveling north from Bethsaida to Caesarea Philipi, *along the way* or in this relationship that they have with Him. In the same way, in this relationship that we have or can have with Him, He calls upon us to decide what we think about Him. First, He asks, "Who do men say I am?" The question has significance in the larger context of Mark's gospel. The plural form "men" in Mark's gospel can designate a kind of category. Consider the following verses:

Follow me and I will make you fishers of men. Mark 1:17

They worship me in vain; their teachings are but rules taught by men.
Mark 7:7-8

…the Son of Man is being betrayed into the hands of men.
Mark 9:31

…who then can be saved? With men it is impossible but not with God. Mark 10:27

…the baptism of John, was it from heaven or from men? Mark 11.30

"Men" describes helpless, hardened, and hostile creatures in need of divine help. The answers the disciples give -John the Baptist or Elijah or some other prophet –are high estimations but miss the point, and humanity is still missing the point today.

According to archaeologists, a temple built by Herod to honor Caesar Augustus as the son of God, was near the road that Jesus and His disciples were taking to Caesarea. Jesus may have asked this question– "Who do men say I am?" - within sight of the temple. Regardless of whether or not this is so, we must consider this question in the shadow of our own looming gods. If you are wondering what a god is, I'll give you this definition: *A god is whatever sits at the very top of the pyramid of your hierarchy of values*. In John 7:37 Jesus says, "Whoever comes to Me and drinks will have living waters flowing from within him." A god is whatever you turn to for vitality or safety. I mean those things that seem to control our destiny and happiness, the temples of our hearts where all sorts of things are worshipped and obeyed. It may be your education. It may be the prospect of marriage or some other precious relationship. It may be whatever the Next Big Thing is that is going to fix everything. It may be something good that I've turned into a god such as my health or happiness. It may be my thinking about gun control or the 2nd Amendment or the Democratic or Republican visions for the nation.

My god is whatever seems like living water to me, whatever makes me feel really alive, full of purpose and direction and meaning when I think or talk about it.

Who Do You Say I Am?

"You are the Christ!" Peter says. Behind the title "Christ" is the Hebrew term that means "anointed one." The priests and kings of the Israel were anointed with oil (Ex.29:7, 21,1Sam.10:1) It carries with it the idea of consecration to God's service, of being chosen by Him for a particular task and endowed by Him with power to fulfill it. In the time of Jesus the term pointed to the ruler who was to restore the kingdom of David to more than its former glory and prosperity.

The title given by Peter designates Jesus as the true meaning and fulfillment of the long succession of Israel's anointed kings and priests. He is the King and Priest whom they all dimly, but, nonetheless, foreshadowed. The good news, though, is that God wants *us* to know Him. Mark's gospel proves this to us as Jesus reveals Himself in the context of this friendship with His disciples.

Our knowledge of one another is largely limited because, sadly, you have to be careful how much you let people know about yourself, don't you? If they become aware of your weakness or secret or what is going on in your home or your heart, they can hurt you.

Apart from the supernatural work of the Holy Spirit, we come to know God in a way that is not unlike how you would come to know anyone. Persons must willingly allow themselves to be known. In the divine relationship with God, He initiates and goes first, revealing and disclosing Himself to us. Then we, in response to His living and giving revelation, trust in Him. We reveal our troubled souls to Him, seeking the comfort only He can give. The amazing thing in this relationship is that this trust in Him transforms and changes us. Paul says it is "at work" in us.

> We also thank God continually because when you received the word of God [the gospel] which you heard from us, you accepted it not as the word of men, but as it actually is, the word of God, which is *at work* in you who believe. 1 Thess.2:13

Without such belief at work in us, we are lost. If we choose not to believe, we still need to hope in something. Consider Stephen Hawking, the renowned physicist, who died recently. The most famous scientist of his generation, Hawking described belief in Christianity and heaven as nothing more than "a fairy story." He was not optimistic about the survival of our planet, and thought we had maybe a thousand years left before our environment collapsed. Since human life will be unsustainable, we'll need to get out of here pretty soon. Humans must, he believed, "continue to go into space for the future of humanity."

For Hawking, humanity's future and hope is in finding new inhabitable worlds. The recent discovery of the Trappist system, 40 light years away and a particular planet in that system named Trappist 1e, was good news for Hawking. He thought it might sustain our kind of life. Hawking was a scientist with tremendous understanding, leaving behind his expansive and influential research on the nature of black holes and much more, but he still needed hope, and he placed it in Trappist 1e. I won't call Trappist 1e a fairy story but our escape to it seems highly unlikely. I believe that Hawking thought what he thought and said what he said because he ruled out the supernatural. He ruled God out, yet still he longed for a kind of future deliverance out of this dying planet to a land light years away, to an inheritance in the stars. In a way, so do I.

We shouldn't be too hard on a brilliant scientist or anyone else for not believing that Jesus is the Son of God. Afterall, such a belief is not natural to any of us.

> Do you not still see or understand? Are your hearts hardened? Do you have eyes but fail to see, and ears but fail to hear? Mark 8:17-18.

Mark has placed these verses in which Jesus's identity is made clear to the disciples just after Jesus tells these same disciples they cannot see or hear. Here is the good news, no, the *great* news for the disciples; for me, and for you: Jesus Christ revealed Himself to them, *and then He stuck with them.* Even though for the last eight chapters He has done miracles, wonders, and signs in their presence, and even though they don't really understand what it all means, He doesn't turn away from them. He doesn't abandon them. He doesn't say, "Enough, I am so done with you!"

What "chapter" is your life or faith in? How many chapters of His mighty works have we already known? And yet the slightest trouble or worry comes along, and we behave as if really don't know who He is or what He is able to do. Are you at the beginning of your faith or several chapters along? Are you thinking about trusting Him? Just starting out? If indeed you do hunger and thirst after the truth, He will hear you when you call out to Him, and He will stay with you until you completely understand who He is. He will stay with you forever, no matter what.

Jesus treats them, and He treats us, just as He treats the blind man of Bethsaida. When we come into a relationship with Him, figuratively speaking, Jesus takes us like He did the blind man *by the hand* (Mark 8:23). His treatment of this man and of us is highly *personal*. I mean that through the power of the Holy Spirit He comes to each of us and gives us His personal attention, performing what amounts to miracle upon miracle. He does not stop giving us attention at the first sign of our ignorance. He works in us until we fully see and understand who He is. Like this blind man and like the disciples, we do not see clearly at first but as Mark tells us, "Once more Jesus put His hands on the man's eyes" (Mark 8:25). It takes more than we realize to finally see. It takes *once more* for all of us.

The Understanding We Need

There is a ferry boat that operates in Long Island Sound. People drive their cars on it, maybe go out on the deck and wait for the crossing to be over. At first glance, there is nothing special about this boat, it is just another ferry boat, one of many they could choose. One day, a retired Long Island Railroad engineer, who had ridden it many times, felt there was something strange he couldn't figure out. Then it came to him. He realized he was riding on an LST – that stands for landing ship tank. LSTs were part of the enormous Allied fleet that crossed the English Channel before dawn on D-Day, June 6, 1944.

We can imagine the associations that would come back to a veteran of D-Day. He realized the true identity of this craft. He was standing on the deck of what to everyone else was just one of the many ferries working the Long Island Sound, but to him it was one of those ships of salvation and suffering; carrying so much liberating and saving power to the captive people of Europe and so many obedient and suffering men who gave up their lives to accomplish it. And it turned out that this was not only an LST, but it was the LST *510*, the very ship on which this man had served.

The world is deceived, lost, false, and depraved, but through the grace of God, through the miracle upon miracle of revelation our eyes are opened. We know that in Jesus Christ we are standing on the deck of divinity, the transport of truth, and that He is the landing ship of salvation for an imprisoned, enslaved, and enthralled world. A new creation is taking place wherever He lands. God give us the grace to scratch down through the paint of our soul's indifference and *behold!* The Apostle Paul says, "If anyone is in Christ, he is a new creation, the old has gone the new has come" (2 Cor.5:17).

O Lord Jesus, Messiah, Son of the living and true God, open my eyes! Touch me once more, as many times as it takes, until I know that the old has gone, and the new has come. This is the understanding I want and the understanding I need.

The Hosanna Moment

Mark 11:1-10

> Those who went ahead and those who followed shouted, "Hosanna!" Blessed is He who comes in the name of the Lord!" Blessed is the coming kingdom of our father, David! Hosanna in the highest!" Mark 11:9-10

Jesus's triumphal entry into Jerusalem, less than a week before His death, is described here in one of the earliest sources of Christian literature, the Gospel of Mark. The Gospels of Matthew and Luke are dependent on Mark. The word the crowd shouted out, "Hosanna," describes a crying out that has gone from *calling and pleading* to *confidence and praising*. The word is a transliteration of a Greek term and the Greek term is a transliteration of the Hebrew. In both English and Greek the term "Hosanna" uses English and Greek letters to make the sound of a Hebrew phrase found in one place in the Old Testament, Psalm 118:25, "Lord, save us!" or "Lord, save please!" You are experiencing a "Hosanna" moment when rescue is needed, and you see that the rescuer has just arrived. In the cry of "Hosanna!" pleading becomes praise.

Imagine you're waiting at the crosswalk of a busy intersection. Across the street, you see a little toddler, unattended, step off the curb into the traffic. You are panicking and crying out, and at that very moment, someone races out to the rescue. Your cry of alarm becomes a cry of praise as you watch the person reaching down to grab the child.

Moses perfectly describes "Hosanna" in the book of Deuteronomy:

> There is none like the God of Israel, who rides on the heavens to help you and on the clouds in His majesty. The eternal God is your refuge, and underneath are the everlasting arms. He will drive out the enemy from before you saying "Destroy him!" Blessed are you, O Israel, Who is like you, a people saved by the Lord? Deut.33:26-27,29a

This is Moses's exclamation of blessing for the congregation of Israel as they traveled to the promised land under the protection of God's name. Many times Moses had experienced God's rescue of the toddler nation. He knew that God's arms were not local or limited, but ever present and ever powerful. In effect, Moses is saying to the people, "Remember always that He showed up when you needed Him and that He answered when you called out to Him for mercy. Remember that You are favored in His eyes and remember that His arms have been there and will always be there ready to reach down, rescue you, and uphold you. His everlasting arms will never tire or fatigue, but will hold you and lift you up."

For Moses and for us, the God of Israel is not a national deity but the sovereign eternal God of *all the world*. This is one of the main points of the Bible. From one perspective, you could summarize the Bible in five sentences, four words each, twenty words total:

1) There is one God.
2) He made our world.
3) We all ruined it.
4) He sent His Son.
5) We all rejected Him.

These themes all come together when Jesus enters Jerusalem, and He is rejected and crucified. This is the setting of the crowd's moment of *Hosanna!* Before looking more closely at their outbreak of joy, consider His rejection that is soon to occur.

Who rejected Jesus?

> The chief priests and the teachers of the law heard this and began looking for a way to kill Him, for they feared Him because the whole crowd was amazed at His teaching. Mark 16:18

In Mark's gospel and in all the gospels, it is the religious leaders who reject Him – "the chief priests and the teachers of the law." Jesus Christ as divine and only Son of God and Savior of the World is rejected by Judaism, rejected by Islam, rejected by most religious studies taught in colleges, schools, institutions, even many churches – rejected by all the religious scholars appearing on most media - NPR, PBS, CBS, NBC, ABC, etc. Of course, they all believe Jesus was an interesting and commanding figure in history, but Son of God? No. Sacrifice for the sins of the world? No. Rescue for sinners? No. Resurrected from the dead? No. Notice perhaps the greatest chapter in John's gospel - the raising of Lazarus from the dead - and how the religious leaders responded in John 11:53: *Then from that day on, they plotted to put Him to death.* Today, that is still what all the religious scholars who regularly make their rounds on the media and talk shows and interviews during Easter season want to do. They want to *put Him to death*, if I could put it that way. Unwittingly perhaps, they want to kill the gospel.

Why were they afraid of Him?

> The chief priests and the teachers of the law heard this and began looking for a way to kill Him, for they feared Him because the whole crowd was amazed at *His teaching*. Mark 11:18

Some people come right out with it and dismiss Jesus entirely – there are people like that; but others do not reject Jesus. They have all kinds of nice things to say about Him but they reject His teaching. They reject the Bible. They fear accountability and want to do as they please. Look back to Mark 7:8-9. Jesus says, "You have let go of the commands of God and are holding on to the traditions of men. You have a fine way of setting aside the commands of God in order to observe your own traditions."

People want to observe their traditions, their values, whatever it is they have imbibed, been taught or caught in their culture. In Jesus's time, of course, this is making reference to rabbinical tradition, but it applies to our own time as well. People are antagonistic toward the Bible – they are antagonistic toward Christ. Anyone who says, "You can't really take the Bible seriously," probably thinks you should take *their* opinions seriously. To be ashamed of the *word of God* is close to being ashamed of the *Son of God*. The rejection of the Scriptures is close to a rejection of Jesus Himself.

Why did He allow Himself to be treated this way?

Jesus is the One whose trust in God and faithfulness to God was greater than any man's trust and faithfulness ever could be. Why did He endure this rejection? By riding on this donkey, by doing what

He was doing, and later on, by allowing Himself to be rejected, Jesus was setting Himself apart from all of humanity.

We do this, too. We set ourselves apart from others, but the difference between us and others is not so great as we think. How different are you and I? It might appear that we are very different, but we're more alike than we are willing to admit. There is probably not a dime's worth of difference between us.

John Stott said, "One of the most extraordinary things Jesus did in his teaching was to set Himself apart from everybody else." Jesus really was different than anyone else. We all have seen ourselves as different from others but there was never anyone who did this so *rightly*, so *completely* and so *correctly* as Jesus Christ. In a way, whenever we think we are better than someone else, we're rejecting Him. From our Lord's point of view, He was the light. Everybody else was darkness. He was the good shepherd. The rest of us were sheep. The world was lost. He wasn't.

To summarize, God sent His Son but the world did, and still does, reject Him. Now we must add a sixth sentence -the gospel - to the five sentence summary of the Bible mentioned earlier.

6) We have a Redeemer.

Jesus's rejection was necessary above all things in order that His sacrifice for our sins be accomplished. The most awful event in history – our rejection of Him and His crucifixion – is made by God to be the most wonderful thing that has ever happened: our salvation. It was God's plan that through our rejection of Him, our salvation would be accomplished at the cross. Peter says,

> This man was handed over to you by God's set purpose and foreknowledge; and you, with the help of wicked men, put Him to death by nailing Him to the cross. But God raised Him from the dead ... Therefore let all Israel be assured of this: God has made this Jesus whom you crucified, both Lord and Christ. Acts 2:23-24,36

God "has made" it this way. He has made all of redemption. We should not think that the idea of atonement by blood is something that naturally developed in history. God ordered it exactly this way. It was God's intention to sacrifice His Son on our behalf so that we might be forgiven. Look at Leviticus 17:11, a single verse that captures all of Leviticus, the entire means of forgiveness in Old Testament, and all of redemption.

> For the life of the creature is in the blood and I have given it to you to make atonement for yourselves on the altar; it is the blood that makes atonement for one's life. Lev. 17:11

Notice the phrase about the blood, "I have given it to you to make atonement." This was God's design and plan. Atonement - being "at one" - is the act by which God restores a relationship of harmony between Himself and us. Our lives have been paid for by the violent death of His Son. As the Apostle Paul says, "In Him we have redemption through His blood" (Eph.1:7). Similarly, the Apostle Peter says, "You were redeemed from the empty way of life handed down to you from your forefathers with ... the precious blood of Christ, a lamb without blemish or defect" (1 Peter 1:18). In dying and then being raised from the dead, He became the source of life and salvation for us.

The Hosanna Moment

Jesus of Nazareth rode into Jerusalem seated on a donkey and was hailed by the crowds who had come to Jerusalem to celebrate the annual Passover feast with shouts of "Hosanna! Blessed is He who comes in the name of the Lord!" The phrase was familiar even if the full meaning of what they shouted was not understood by them. Humanity's cry for help, our need for rescue, turned to praise and joy. The Savior had arrived.

The people in the crowd probably had different ideas than Jesus about the kingdom and what it was. Some of them may have been hoping for the overthrow of their Roman oppressors, the political system they were under. But the Kingdom of God was not an earthly, political kingdom. It is the rule of God in the hearts of people who know and serve Him. This was not the kingdom which the people expected or wanted, and so they rejected Jesus as their Lord.

Sometimes my life and your life is like this. We shout out my praise but when things do not go as we expect, we're not so happy. We don't get the relationship we expected. We don't get the job we expected or the marriage we expected. We don't get the grades we expected. We don't get the life we expected. God does not fulfill our expectations! You are not the congregation I expected. I am not the pastor you expected. We have not lived up to each other's expectations. What if God were in all of this doing something more beautiful than we think, working all things for the good of those who love Him (Rom. 8:28)?

In the painting, *Jesus is Welcomed to Jerusalem* by Pietro Lorenzetti (ca. 1280-1348), the buildings in the background are presumably from the artist's home in Siena, Italy. The crowd is in the path before us. One detail to notice is a man stepping directly in front, spreading his robe on the road, a sign of respect. The man who kneels before Jesus in this painting may be Lorenzetti including himself in the painting. We can't be sure. But we should put *ourselves* in this frame. The Messiah could have come charging into the world on a mighty horse of battle, with sword drawn to judge the earth just as He was expected by Israel's teachers to come. Figuratively speaking, God could have justifiably run over the human race a long time ago. Instead He comes this way, into the traffic of the world, harmless, gentle, bringing peace and salvation. We need to accept Him and welcome Him because "at just the right time, when we were still powerless, Christ died for the ungodly" (Rom.5:8). In Jesus, God came to our rescue at just the right time. And if we believe, here is what must accompany our Hosanna moment: to allow Him to do with us and our lives now as it pleases *Him*, to welcome Him by taking off our expectations and disappointments. Lay them all down before Him. Hosanna, Lord Jesus! Walk on all these expectations, and use everything else in my life as it pleases You, and be glorified.

One Messenger Left to Send

Mark 12:1-12

> He had one left to send, a son he loved. He sent him last of all, saying, "They will respect my son." Mark 12:6

This parable follows the refusal of the Pharisees to consider the source of Christ's authority (Mark 11:27-32). He compares them to the tenants who reject the son of the vineyard's owner. They refused to acknowledge what they feared was true – that Jesus was the Son of God. The parable gives us a picture not only of how the religious establishment of Israel rejected God, but also the general condition of all of fallen humanity. Until and unless we experience the grace of God, we will refuse to acknowledge His authority over us, even though in our hearts we know it is true. The rejection of God portrayed here is not simply a circumstance of history, but the result and proof of our fallen nature.

God's Blessings and Care

> A man planted a vineyard. He put a wall around it, dug a pit for the winepress and built a watchtower. Then he rented the vineyard to some farmers and went away on a journey. Mark 12:1

The vineyard is Israel, God is the owner, and the tenants are the religious leaders of Israel (c.f. Isaiah 5:1-7). There was no doubt about Jesus's comparison. Nearby to where Jesus and this group were standing was the vast door of the temple that led to the Holy Place. Sculpted around this door was a grapevine covered in gold leaf. The bunches of grapes which hung from it were made out of jewels. This is an ideal set of circumstances, a really sweet deal, a perfect situation. The owner has done all the heavy lifting and hard work. He plants the vineyard which means he cleared the land. He builds a tower for whomever will be caring for it. He builds a vat for the storage of the wine. This is a turn key operation. Everything has been completed for a succesful and properous enterprise. Do some of you recognize this? Would I be wrong in saying to you that the same Lord has been so gracious to you? His blessings are so great, and there is so much protection and care and love you have received in life!

His Patience and Grace

> At harvest time he sent a servant to the tenants to collect from them some of the fruit of the vineyard. But they seized him, beat him and sent him away empty-handed. Then he sent another servant to them; they struck this man on the head and treated him shamefully. He sent still another, and that one they killed. He sent many others; some of them they beat, others they killed.   Mark 12:2-5

God displayed patience and forbearance with Israel and still does with us and all the world. He sent Moses. He sent Samuel. He sent Elijah. He sent Elisha. He sent Isaiah. He sent Jeremiah and Ezekiel and Daniel and Hosea, Joel, Amos, Obadiah, Jonah, Micah, Nahum, Habbakuk, Zephaniah, Haggai, Zechariah, and Malachi. God sent the prophets to test the loyalty and obedience that the people should have wanted to readily give to the One who had blessed them and given them all they had. These messengers were all rejected. His patience and forbearance which ought to have lead to repentance, instead, provoked sinful rebellion.

Hasn't God been good to you? But we can be so resentful and bitter toward Him, some of us our whole life. His kindness, like the wonderful parents you have; your husband; your wife; your children or grandchildren; your sons and daughters who came back from the war; your long years of health; the prosperity you have known; it all has come from God. Remember the time you almost died but incredibly you're here alive! You survived cancer and disease. You've lived to an old age. What mercies you've had from God! But will you read the Bible? Will you pray? Will you obey God? Will you confess your sins to God? Will you seek the provision of the blood of Christ to protect you? No. Yet God continues to be good to you. Will you love the Lord? No. God's patience just leads to further rebellion against Him. You're stubborn.

Our Stubborn Hearts

> Or do you show contempt for the riches of His kindness, tolerance, and patience, not realizing that God's kindness leads you toward repentance? But because of your stubbornness of heart and your unrepentant heart, you are storing up wrath for yourself, when His righteous judgment will be revealed. Rom. 2:4-5

Consider Paul's words as we read through this parable. The behavior of the tenants seems *inexplicably* violent. They beat people, throw stones at them, treat others shamefully, kill others and finally kill the son. Why are they like this? Our attention is on the tenants and their wickedness in mistreating and even killing the messengers. They are the religious leaders of Israel. As we read of what they are doing, we shake our heads in disbelief. Why would they, or how could they, be so mean and foolish? It is hard for us to understand such evil characters. But that is just the way sin is. It is a disposition or inclination toward evil that should not surprise us. It is human nature. And no matter how much good we ourselves might do or might see done in the world, we all probably understand what Jesus means when he says that no one is good but God (Mark 9:18).

A modern psychologist might ask: Is the tenants' behavior dispositional or situational? You may know about the Stanford University experiment in the early 70s. A group of social scientists created a mock prison in the basement of the psychology building. They were trying to find out why prisons are such horrible places. Half of the people were made guards, the other half were prisoners. The local police helped out by agreeing to "arrest" those designated as prisoners in their homes; handcuff them, blindfold them, and bring them to the prison. Was it the environment or the people that made it bad? As the experiment progressed, the guards became increasingly cruel and sadistic and the prisoners became increasingly withdrawn and hysterical. They intended for the experiment to run a couple of weeks, but shut it down after six days. The truth about human nature is that no matter how bad the situation is, we can always go lower! If Jesus's story of the vineyard were a psychology experiment, it would also be one for the books.

William Wilberforce, the 19th century British statesman who led the campaign to abolish the slave trade, writes,

> These facts are certain; they cannot be disputed... though these effects of human depravity are every where acknowledged and lamented, we must not expect to find

them traced to their true origin. Prepare yourself to hear rather of frailty and infirmity, of petty transgressions, of occasional failings…and of such other qualifying terms as may serve to keep out of view the true source of the evil. The bulk of professed Christians speak of man as of a being who, naturally pure, and inclined to all virtue, is sometimes, almost involuntarily, drawn out of the right course, or is overpowered by the violence of temptation. Vice, with them, is rather an accidental and temporary, than a constitutional and habitual distemper; a noxious plant, which, though found to live, and even to thrive in the human mind, is not the natural growth and production of the soil. It is all in the soil of our soul.

His point is that we do not want to admit how bad off we are, and that our own hearts are the source of our troubles.

We have all done some landscaping. We've dug and shaped the earth. We covered over the ground with decorative gravel and lined the edges with rock. It is very attractive. But then the weeds come up! How did that happen!? No matter what it looks like, there is still dirt underneath it all. This is how the Bible wants us to understand our disposition towards sin. Are we surprised by the sin in our life or in others' lives? There is the dirt of depravity that provides all the right nutrients for the weeds. We might have an attractively landscaped life, but when the weeds of sin come up, we shouldn't be surprised because there is all of this dirt underneath whatever we do, underneath the manicured apearance. What is the solution?

One Messenger Left to Send

> He had one left to send, a son, whom he loved. He sent him last of all, saying, 'They will respect my son.' But the tenants said to one another,'This is the heir. Come, let's kill him, and the inheritance will be ours.' So they took him and killed him, and threw him out of the vineyard. What then will the owner of the vineyard do? He will come and kill those tenants and give the vineyard to others. Mark 12:6-8

The passage shows what will happen to those who were planning and plotting Jesus's death. It highlights the importance of what we do with Jesus. The tenants kill the heir, not because they do not recognize Him, but because they know exactly who He is. We have no excuse. Christ is rejected not because we do not know who He is. We should, and do know. Look at the stunning sequel a few verses down, from Psalm 118: "The stone the builders rejected has become the capstone; the Lord has done this, and it is marvelous in our eyes" (Mark12:10). In other words, the builders, who have the professional capacity to understand building, construction, and stones, are without excuse. They have rejected the stone they should have easily recognized.

Psalm 118, quoted here, is probably making immediate reference to King David himself and how all the great leaders and kings of the earth did not see his significance (even the prophet Samuel was not very impressed with David at first). But God would reveal David's importance. Now with the Jesus and His death and resurrection, this Psalm is being fulfilled by one of David's descendants. Just as the Apostle Paul writes:

> ...the gospel He promised beforehand through His prophets in the Holy Scriptures regarding His Son, who as to human nature was a descendant of David, and who through the Spirit of holiness was declared with power to be the Son of God by His resurrection from the dead: Jesus Christ our Lord. Through Him and for His name's sake we have received grace... and you also are among those who are called to belong to Jesus Christ. Rom.1:1-6

We understand Him perfectly, and that is why we reject Him. A few Jews crucified Him, but by their actions the whole world rejected and killed Him. The world judged Jesus unfit to live and gave Him a pauper's grave. It is as if any one of you could reach into the pocket of your sport coat or reach into your purse right now and you could pull out the very nails used in His crucifixion. That is how responsible we all are. With all the mistakes the Pharisees made, there is one mistake that we might make that they did not make. Look in verse 12: "They knew He had spoken the parable against them." They realized it. But do you know this is spoken against *you*? It is, if you reject Him! If you are not a Christian or if you think of yourself as a Christian but you have turned your back on Him, this is spoken against you. But now, isn't it marvelous in your eyes? Paul says that "you also are among those who are called to belong to Jesus Christ."

The One the tenants rejected is really the only One they must receive, and if they receive Him, all can be put right. He is "last of all" (v.6). Jesus is the last of the prophets. No more prophets were ever again sent from heaven. No Mohammed, no Joseph Smith, no Charles Taze Russell, no Ted Armstrong, no Sun Myung Moon, no Ron Hubbard, no Maharishi Yogi, none of them was sent from heaven. Jesus Christ is the true and last prophet. He left nothing unsaid that His Father gave Him to say. No other prophets are needed. The Lord Jesus is the all sufficient prophet. If you reject God's messenger there isn't another one coming. This is the One that we must really receive. You have known God's blessings and patience and forebearance, but this is His last messenger to you! This is the only way your evil heart can be helped and healed. Receive and recognize Him now before He returns to judge the world and all those who have rejected Him. After all you have done against God, against others, for all your wrong, for all your sin, the acceptance of this messenger can put everything right. There is no other way, but this way. It is open to you.

The Greatest Commandment Ever Told

Mark 12:28-34

> When Jesus saw that he had answered wisely, He said to him, "You are not far from the kingdom of God." Mark 12:34

Have you watched that old Alfred Hitchcock film *The Man Who Knew Too Much?* It's about a guy who learns of a plot to assassinate an important government official and how his family is drawn into this plot. His son is kidnapped by the people planning the crime so they can threaten him and keep him quiet. Eventually, he and his wife foil the assassination attempt, rescue their son, and amazingly it all works out. They live happily ever after!

The Man Who Knew So Much

In our text is a man who knew *so* much. But it isn't exactly a happy ending, is it? Jesus tells him, "You're not far from the kingdom of God." He was *near* it, but not *in* it. He knew so much. He had heard Jesus. He was in His presence and valued His answer. Maybe from that time on he even repeated those words to his family and friends. But he himself was not in the kingdom of God. He was at the border but had not crossed over into it.

Imagine traveling to the beach on a hot day, anticipating running into the water, but a few miles from the beach your car breaks down. You have to wait there the whole day while the tow truck comes. You never make it to the beach. It is really no consolation that you are close to it.

This man was a devout man, a smart and intelligent man. He was a teacher. He probably knew that the rabbis of his era taught that there were 615 commandments in their Torah or 365 'Thou shalt nots' and 250 'Thou shalts.' Yet with all his respectability, intelligence, devotion, even though he understood the answer of Jesus was correct, he was outside the kingdom. Jesus's words were written down by Mark, and he doesn't want us to hurry over them and ignore them. I might have all the right "doctrine," and I might even have great moments of enlightenment and understanding, but still be outside the kingdom.

He Knew that We Should Love God

> One of the teachers of the law came and heard them debating. Noticing that Jesus had given them a good answer, he asked Him, "Of all the commandments which is the most important one?" " The most important one," answered Jesus, "is this, 'Hear O Israel, the Lord our God, the Lord is One. Love the Lord your God with all your heart and with all your soul and with all your mind and with all your strength.'" Mark 12:28-30

Jesus answers the question with Deuteronomy 10:4. He speaks about love for God. It is not so much about our actions as it is about the heart, the attitude, or the affection that motivates our behavior. Love for God means loving Him emotionally, intellectually, enduringly. Consider these verses:

> Take careful heed to yourselves that you love the Lord your God. Joshua 23:11

> Let those who love Him be like the sun when it comes out in full strength. Judges 5:31

To love God means that I am willing to hear His words of judgment against me as well as His words of hope for me. To love God means that I grasp and accept His sternness with His encouragement; His holiness with His grace; His absolute intolerance of my sin with His inconceivable and divine patience towards me. Loving God in truth from the heart is more important than any kind of ceremony or sacrifice (Hosea 6:6; Micah 6:6-8). This man knew that we should love God but he also understood *why* we should love Him.

And He Knew Why We Should Love God

> "Well said, teacher," the man replied. "You are right in saying the Lord our God is One and there is no other but Him." Mark 12:32

This is from Deuteronomy 6:4. And we need to know this, too. Like this man and like the ancient Israelites, we must grasp the absolute sovereignty of our God. For Jesus this is the foremost thing we must know. It is about His position and place over all creation, not simply over the Jews, but all of the world.

> Is He the God of the Jews only? Is He not also the God of the Gentiles? Yes, of the Gentiles also, since there is one God who will justify the circumcised by faith and the uncircumcised by that same faith. Rom. 3:29-30.

There are many competing and powerful forces in our lives. So many things seem to matter, and those things can seem very god-like. But the only way is that you should begin, continue, and end in life is knowing that God is One; and knowing the love of the sovereign and majestic power of God over all, God Almighty, King of kings, Lord of lords. He is *your* God. "The Lord has established His throne in heaven, and His kingdom rules over all" (Psalm 103:19). This why we should love Him, because of His rule and care for us throughout all creation. He is God and there is no other. He is ruling over your life. Jesus often dismissed Pharisees and teachers of the law as "hypocrites" and "blind guides," but this man seems to understand something and Jesus tells him, "You are not far from the kingdom of God." There is hope in these words, isn't there? How could he get in? We don't know what happened to him after this, but we can know about ourselves. How can *we* get in? We need to know and recognize the truth.

The Truth that Matters So Much

> While Jesus was teaching in the temple courts, He asked, "How is it that the teachers of the law say that the Christ is the son of David? David himself, speaking by the Holy Spirit, declared: 'The Lord said to my Lord: Sit at my right hand until I put your enemies under your feet.' David himself, calls him 'Lord.' How can this be His son?" The crowd listened to Him with delight. Mark 12:35-37

We don't know if the man who questioned Jesus in Mark 12:28 was listening when Jesus spoke later from Psalm 110. Psalm 110 was of great importance to the early church and preachers. It was written by King David. Jesus is making a very simple but decisive point. The teachers of the law believed that the Messiah would descend from David, and Jesus's question is this: In what sense is this true that the Messiah is the son of David? He uses Psalm 110 to demonstrate that the Messiah is *more* than just a descendant of David. After all, Jesus points out, look at what David himself says. David calls Him, "LORD". The point that Jesus is making is that the Messiah is the son of David, yes, but not *merely* the son of David. He also has an exalted role. He is David's descendant, yes, and therefore his "junior," but in some mysterious and wonderful way, Jesus points out, He is also superior to David, He is also "LORD." David died and did not ascend to rule in heaven, but David's descendant reigns, as it says, "Sit at my right hand until I put your enemies under your feet." Believing in Jesus as *Lord* -the same name given to God- as the One who came and died, now risen and reigning, this is how we come into the kingdom.

As noted above, with their understanding of the Torah, the Jews, in a way, had come up with approximately 615 problems. What should I avoid doing? What should I do? What is the most important thing that I need to do? Sometimes I feel like I have 615 problems, give or take a few. You might not really feel you have any problems. You might have a lot of the right doctrine, the right family, the right job, the right outcome from all your income. Maybe you have some great moments of enlightenment and understanding. But unless you believe in Jesus Christ as the dying and resurrected Lord, the just One who died for the unjust, the One who came from heaven to foil the devil and to ransom you from the captivity of your sins, unless you believe this is true, you have a big problem. You are spiritually dead.

The point Jesus is making is that it is not about what we do or do not do. And it doesn't matter if I feel I have a lot of problems or feel that I have none. Here is the truth that matters so much: Do I believe that Jesus is Lord over all? Do I believe that His death was punishment for the way I have lived or not lived? Do I understand that the just One died for me, the unjust? Do I believe that He did this so that I might experience the grace that gives me a complete change of heart towards God? Has God given to me a new birth from above? Unless this happens, the world will be just so many gods demanding my affection and worship. Why not ask Him today, "Lord, what is the most important thing of all?" He will tell you what He says here - *Love the Lord your God with all your heart and with all your soul and with all your mind and with all your strength!*

The Greatest Commandment Ever Told (2)

Mark 12:28-34

> The second is this: 'Love your neighbor as yourself.' Mark 12:31

Once, a reporter asked Thomas Edison during an interview, "Do you think it will ever be possible to construct an instrument to discover and to exhibit our thoughts against our neighbor?" Edison answered, "Such an instrument is possible but what then? Every man would flee from the face of his neighbor."

How very frightening and alarming it would be if such an invention actually did exist. What if, in our own modern social media era, you could download such an app for your phone? Imagine that you are sitting with a friend for coffee, or let's say, out on a first date with someone. You are making casual conversation and, without you knowing it, the other person turns on the new Omniscience app. It gives them access to your thoughts about them. That would probably end of a lot of relationships. Aren't you glad no one has come up with such an app yet? What a relief. But if we read the Bible and believe in God we should still be frightened about our thoughts toward our neighbor. The thoughts I manage to keep hidden from view, God completely knows. They are not hidden from Him.

I am told here that I must love my neighbor as myself. This man asks Jesus a question, and we looked at this passage, first, to understand the importance of our love for God. We're coming back to it to look at the other part of Jesus's answer.

The Greatest Commandment

> Love the Lord your God with all your heart, and with all your soul, and with all your mind and with all your strength, Jesus tells them the man, but He doesn't stop there He goes on: The second is this: 'Love your neighbor as yourself.' There is no commandment greater than these. Mark 12:30-31

If we understand what Jesus says here, it is overwhelming. The instinct I have for self-preservation, self-care, self-esteem – all the longings I have for myself, I must now feel for others *as if they were me*. In some way, I must feel that I am that other person. If that is correct something very remarkable must happen to me. For me to fulfill the Greatest Commandment would require the *Greatest Invention* of all time because I have the Greatest Problem.

The Greatest Problem

> When Jesus saw that he had answered wisely, He said to him, "You are not far from the kingdom of God." Mark 12:34.

As noted in the previous sermon, this man – a teacher of the law- was close to the kingdom but not *in*. Jesus speaks in the strongest terms at times condemning the Scribes and Pharisees because they are so antagonistic, but He encourages this man. He tells him that he is not far from the kingdom of God. There was still in this man, as we might find sometimes in people we meet, a nearness to the kingdom, but also a critical failure of recognizing who Jesus is. He is LORD. Like so many of his time and our time, this man probably thought that his behavior just needed a little more effort on his part.

You can be a really wise person in so many ways, and, in a way, the best of all people, best of all fathers, the best of all mothers, the best of all teenagers, the best of all workers, the best of all employers or businesses, the best of all teachers, the best of all friends. We can be the best of all, but still not be in the kingdom of God. J.C. Ryle says,

> Let's put away the common notion that seeing and knowing what is good is enough to make a man a Christian. The great experiment has been made in the instance of the Jewish nation . . . nothing but the Spirit of God can change the heart. We must be born again.

In the Old Testament there is a story that makes this point in a memorable way. It takes place in 2 Kings 2:19-22. The men of a certain city go to Elisha with a complaint.

> "Please notice, the situation of this city is pleasant, as my lord sees, but the water is bad, and the ground barren." And he said, "Bring me a new bowl, and put salt in it." So they brought it to him. Then he went out to the source of the water, and cast in the salt there, and said, "Thus says the Lord: 'I have healed this water; from it there shall be no more death or barrenness.'" 2Kings 2:19-22

We are like this. The old way of dependence on ourselves will not work. Faith in Jesus Christ and understanding the gospel is like this "new bowl," cleansing us at the fountain head of the heart, not a half mile downstream in our deeds. Love for God must come first. Only when we have this kind of love poured into our heart, like salt in a spring, can what flows from it be sweet. Jesus is offering to pour in the salt. The cross of Christ is God's greatest invention. Look at the next few verses.

The Greatest "Invention"

David himself speaking by the Holy Spirit, declared, " 'The Lord said to my Lord, 'Sit at My right hand, until I put Your enemies under Your feet.' " Mark 12:36

You can read a more careful explanation of these verses in the previous sermon, but what Jesus means here is that on the basis of Psalm 110, the Messiah is more than a descendant of David. Even though the Messiah comes after David who is His ancestor, He is superior and above David. In pointing this out, Jesus, as the Messiah, is claiming to be David's LORD, our LORD or THE LORD of heaven and earth and the One to whom all will be subordinated. When you believe this about Him, that He is the Son of God, very God of God, the Lord who came to die for our sins and was raised from the grave, God will hear you. He will pour the purifying salt of the Savior into your bitter heart, into your life, and into all of your relationships. This is God's greatest invention. Listen to what Paul writes in Romans 8:3-4,

> For what the law was powerless to do in that it was weakened by the sinful nature, God did by sending His own Son in the likeness of sinful man to be a sin offering. And so He condemned sin in sinful man in order that the righteous requirements of the law might be fully met in us who not do live according to the sinful nature [i.e., depending on ourselves] but according to the spirit [i.e., depending on Christ].

We fulfill the law now—loving our neighbor as we love ourselves—not through our power but by the power of the Holy Spirit. It is not that we love others *instead* of ourselves. We love others as we love ourselves when walk in the Holy Spirit. As Paul says elsewhere in Galatians, "The entire law is summed up in a single command: Love your neighbor as yourself" (Galatians 5:14). Paul is talking pretty close to home. He is not talking about loving people we will never meet or praying for people we will never know, but people close to us. We are enabled by the Spirit of God to love each other. A variety of things are possible through the Spirit.

> But the fruit of the Spirit is love, joy, peace, patience, kindness, goodness, faithfulness, gentleness, self-control. Gal. 5:22-23

The fruit of the Spirit is not something abstract. Having been set free you can now think in new ways. You have new "apps" for your soul that can help you respond to your family, to your friends, to everyone. If we say we love God, we must love those who bear His image.

People will say they love someone, but you know when they are serious. I know a man in St. Louis who loves Bob Dylan. Lots of people will say they love Bob Dylan. With him there's no doubt. How do I know? He has all of Bob Dylan's records, more than thirty of them, lined up going all the way back to 1962. He had never even seen Bob Dylan but you know he loves him *because of the way he cares for his recordings*. Grooved into each of these records is the unmistakeable image of the artist, each bearing Dylan's creative genius.

Our relationship to God is no different. We can say we love Him, but it is only proven if and when we love those who are the records of His work. Sometimes the actions of others will call simply for love, choosing to love them instead of hating them. Or it may call for being joyful because of their advantages rather than being jealous. You might need to be a peacemaker when they're a troublemaker. You might need to exhibit patience in the face of an insult or a slight. We might need to answer harshness with kindness. We might need to answer their evil with goodness, or their flakiness with our own faithfulness. When we love others in these ways, this is how our love for God is seen.

Even when a record is horribly scratched you can still listen to it and distinguish the artist. The world has scratched us all up badly. We might not feel like we belong in anyone's collection. The world, like a turntable with a bad needle, has played us round and round and used us up and worn us out. God commands us to collect one another up and treasure His image and gifts. This is what Jesus transforms us to do through the power of the cross, to love those who bear the undeniable image of the Artist who made us all.

The Victory He Secured

Mark 16:1-20

> After the Lord Jesus had spoken to them, He was taken up in heaven and He sat at the right hand of God. Mark 16:19

In our reading Mark recounts what happened at the resurrection, just as he did with Jesus's death and burial. The time, the day, the details of the preparation, the problem of removing the stone, the fact that it *is* removed, the repeated confirmation that the body of Jesus is gone, even the reference to meeting him in Galilee – all this demonstrates that Mark intends us to take the resurrection as a historical reality. There is no place for the idea that the resurrection is a metaphor, a picture representing new hope, or a mere story born of the disciples' determination to carry on the ministry and message of Jesus after His death. To the contrary, after the crucifixion the disciples seem defeated, and are simply trying to stay out of sight and keep their heads down. The idea that the resurrection did not really happen is completely alien to the New Testament writers, all of whom were fully convinced that these events happened, and most of whom were eye witnesses. Our faith stands and falls by them.

On this resurrection Sunday, "Let us fix our eyes on Jesus, the author and finisher of our faith, who for the joy set before Him endured the cross, scorning its shame, and sat down at the right hand of throne of God" (Heb.12:2). Christ has endured the cross, and now it is transformed from the symbol of death into a symbol of life for us. It is like a line from a poem by William Cowper, "They whom Truth and Wisdom lead can gather honey from a weed." That is what Jesus

Christ has done with the cross. He has gathered "honey from a weed." He has gotten the *honey* of salvation *from the weed* of the cross. So much of what we learn about the resurrection of Jesus gathers honey from a weed.

The Women at the Resurrection

> When the Sabbath was over, Mary Magdalene, Mary the mother of James, and Salome brought spices so that they might anoint Jesus's body. Mark 16:1

All four of the gospels record that the first to receive the news of Christ's resurrection were women. None of the Twelve were first. This is one feature of all the gospel accounts which goes a long way demonstrating the authenticity of Christ's resurrection. Skeptics of the resurrection have suggested the whole event was fabricated by the early church after Jesus's death. But if it were true that the church and disciples made all this up, the accounts would not have included these women. Their culture was one in which women were considered inferior to men. They would have been easily and frequently discredited. Why would Jewish men of this era invent a story that relied upon the testimony of women? I believe the unexpected role of women as witnesses of Jesus's resurrection foreshadows the unfolding recognition of their equality to men in the church and society (c.f. Joel 2:28; Acts 2:17-18; Gal. 3:28). Regardless of whether I'm right or not, these three women in Mark's account are intricately woven into these events as the *primary* witnesses. What they saw, heard, and spoke turned the darkest day in history into the greatest story ever told.

The Astonishment of the Resurrection

> Trembling and bewildered, the women went out and fled from the tomb. They said nothing to anyone because they were afraid. Mark 16:8

It is not an exaggeration to say that there was not one single person on earth who expected Jesus to rise that Sunday morning. Anyone can be executed, but not anyone can emerge from a grave a few days later. The word translated "bewildered" suggests a combination of astonishment and amazement and terror. It's disturbing enough to find the tomb open and someone sitting inside, but the women are far beyond surprise. It is dread and terror that they feel because they recognize that this is no ordinary young man, but an angel. And the words spoken by the angel - "He is risen! He is not here"- transform their lives forever, and add further astonishment to their fear. They are in such a state of amazement that they are befuddled. God is turning all human expectations upside down! Mark's ending doesn't even allow that the women did as they were instructed by the angel- "Go, tell his disciples and Peter." They do eventually recover themselves, as we know from the other accounts, and go to the disciples and Peter to tell them what has happened. But here the emphasis is on how completely undone and overwhelmed they are by what has taken place. You and I, reading this story, ought to wonder and feel something of that disturbance. Something unpredictable, astonishing, and really quite unthinkable, has happened.

The Meaning of the Resurrection

> After the Lord Jesus had spoken to them, He was taken up in heaven and He sat at the right hand of God. Then

the disciples went out and preached everywhere, and the Lord worked with them and confirmed the word by the signs that accompanied it. Mark 16:19-20

The belief that Jesus rose from the dead is of no value unless we understand what it *means*. You have to understand the meaning of His death, and you have to understand the meaning of His Resurrection. If you simply believe that Jesus rose to life, amazing as that is, all you have is a happy ending to a sad story. Make sure you understand His death. By going to the cross and dying, He received the punishment for our sins. He had to be "crushed for our iniquities" (Isaiah 53:5). The King James Version says, "bruised for our iniquities." He was crushed or bruised so that when we look to Him in faith God's forgiveness can be a reality because Jesus has taken the punishment. Jesus has paid it all.

A friend of mine recently had a very bad fall. I was surprised to see him up and around just a few days afterwards. He greeted me. He was smiling and cheerful. He seemed fine. But then I glanced down and noticed his left arm and hand. They were terribly bruised, discolored, and swollen. The rest of him looked great, like nothing had happened. He explained to me that when he had fallen, he had thrust out his left arm to protect himself. His left arm had born all the impact of the fall. It looked awful and very painful. He could hardly move it.

If you are a Christian, despite your sin, despite the Fall, despite the troubles of your life, look at you today! Here you are smiling and cheerful. Why? Because you know that Jesus Christ is God's *arm* of salvation. God saw humanity's fall into sin coming before the foundation of the world and He planned the death of His only Son.

He thrust Him, like an arm, into harm's way, so that all the weight of our sin might be entirely on Jesus. This is the meaning of Christ's death. In a way, despite what has happened to all of us, we look pretty good because He took the bruising for us. Belief in the resurrection likewise has no value unless we understand what it means. It is not just an exciting or happy ending, it means that sin and death and evil is defeated. Death is the proof of our ruin, proof of our sin, proof of the great calamity and systemic evil that lurks in this world and our hearts and our minds, but Jesus who was crushed for us has now crushed death and great power is now ours. That is made clear in the patchwork of events and stories that are added throughout the ending of Mark's gospel. Jesus gives His disciples power through the Holy Spirit over evil and sickness so that in those beginning times of their proclamation the world would sit up and take notice.

The Victory of the Resurrection

There is a single word that sums up Mark's ending. It is not a word found in our text, but a word that generates more joy, relief, and tears of happiness than perhaps any other word in all the world. The word is VICTORY. If they could broadcast an Easter special from heaven, every saint would want you to know this. If in such a program they lost the audio signal for a moment, they would only need to lift up their hands and flash you the V for Victory. Jesus is alive. Victory over death! The forgiveness of sins has been accomplished. He is risen, and given everyone who believes in Him the promise and hope of the resurrection, too.

The V for victory is flashing and there is something more. Mark is making it clear that Jesus isn't physically around anymore, but something tremendous has started. He is risen and His followers are now coping with the reality that He isn't physically present. They are dealing with His absence, until the day when He returns. That is what we are all doing if we trust in Christ. We are dealing with His absence. He has sent His Spirit, yes, to empower us to go and proclaim, but we are still waiting for Him. We don't have to go into the exact details mentioned in Mark's ending. He generally suggests how we ought to cope: we have work to do. Until He returns we must learn to offer our bodies as living sacrifices and live for Him (Rom. 12:1). We have people to forgive. We have people to love. We have people to visit. We have people to care about. We have tears to shed. We have work to do and sweat to offer. We have relationships to mend. We have struggles. We have sins. We have troubles. We have doubt, depression, divorce, disease, and death. But there is victory over it all because His is risen, and He is coming again! As Jesus says "At that time men will see the Son of Man coming in clouds with great power and glory" (Mark 13:26). What a day that will be when we finally get to the end of what He started on that day.

If you ever watch the Grand Ole Opry, you notice something about the crowd. When the band is playing and the singer is singing, they don't wait for the song to end before they applaud. If they like it, they start clapping and whistling, right in the middle of the performance. With Christ's resurrection, the song of redemption has begun. We are in the middle, but we could rejoice right now. Death has been defeated. What do you think of that song? Sin is overcome. Do you like that song? Forgiveness is accomplished! If you believe in Him, your life has purpose. Do you like the song? He has work, glorious work, for you to do. Don't wait until the end to rejoice.

Hannah's Treasure

1 Samuel 1-2:1

> Then Hannah prayed and said, "My heart rejoices in the Lord; in the Lord my horn is lifted high." 1 Samuel 2:1

The Hebrew name, "Hannah" means "grace" or "favor." What can we learn from gracious Hannah about God?

Hannah Teaches Us to Treasure the Person of God.

Hannah had a conscious relationship with God. 1 Samuel 1:12 says, "she kept on praying to the Lord." We need this, too. In 2:1, her prayer begins this way, "My heart rejoices in the Lord." The very name by which she calls Him, "Lord," stands out. Don't overlook this in her prayer or in your own prayer. When you use that title for God, it means something. You cannot call Him "Lord" and not love Him. You cannot call Him "Lord" and remain unaware of His love for you. Perhaps her sorrow drove her more deeply into a true and lasting relationship with God, beyond simply calling him God or the "God of Israel," as Eli the priest and everyone else called God. She called him, "Lord," the name for God that carries so much *relational* power. Do you have that relationship with Him? All that she thinks, does, and says is centered in the great act of God in her life. It is that relational power that is described here in 2:1, "In the Lord my horn is lifted high."

She had been bowed down in her barreness but now like a mighty stag, she was rearing her horn "in the Lord." This image of the horn being lifted up is like the image of a deer with antlers raised up in a display of strength. She was a weak and barren woman in a male-dominated society, but *in the Lord* she was a mighty force and the world and the world's woes could not overcome her. She had given birth to one who was to be used by God to affect a great change, to bring about a new day, a new era for Israel. This promise of David's kingdom filled her with joy and strength and thanksgiving.

She Teaches Us to Treasure the Presence of God.

Look at 1 Samuel 1:20. Hannah conceived and bore a son and called him Samuel. 1 Samuel 1:24 goes on to say, "After he was weaned, she took the boy with her, young as he was, along with a three-year-old bull, an ephah of flour, and a skin of wine, and brought him to the house of the Lord at Shiloh." Hannah was very happy on this occasion, wasn't she? She was filled with joy. But this was not the first time she had been to Shiloh. Hannah knew that Shiloh was the place to go when she was *hurting*, too. She went to the house of the Lord at Shiloh when her heart was filled with misery (1 Samuel 1:7,9). Shiloh, according to Jeremiah 7:12, was the place where the Lord dwelt. It was site of the tabernacle and His presence, His dwelling place (c.f. Joshua 18:1).

The Lord's presence is desirable in the low points of life. It may be easier to be in a worship service when you are happy, and all the bills are paid and none of your children are in jail. But let a little misery creep into your life and suddenly the idea of coming into a worship service and risking that your circumstances and emotions might be exposed is not so appealing. How about that Christmas letter or the annual letter that so many families send out ? You don't send one of those. Things aren't so rosy. Your daughter is having a baby, but she isn't married. Your son is in rehab. You don't feel like going to church, facing all the got-no-troubles smiles and hearing all that joy. That is why we need to consider Hannah. When she was miserable, she went willingly to Shiloh. She went to the house of the Lord. She knew then what we ought to know now from Hebrews 4:16:

> Let us then approach the throne of grace with confidence, so that we may receive mercy and find grace to help us in our time of need.

In the presence of God, through Jesus Christ, grace is on the throne. Come to the Lord's presence when you are hurting. To put it another way, it should be okay to be miserable in church. In fact, it might be good and even important for all of us to have some misery to draw us closer to God; to keep us genuine and in touch with one another. It tells us in 1 Samuel 1:9-12 that one time in Shiloh, Hannah just stood up and was in "bitterness of soul" and "wept very much." Eli watches her. He thinks she is drunk. That must have happened. People got drunk at Shiloh. Eli is just trying to keep order. The point to make here is that the presence of God- wherever and whenever you seek His presence -is a place for weeping.

Many of the churches of America in the 18th century - and I don't mean only the more outwardly expressive and emotional Pentecostal or charismatic churches, but churches of all denominations - were places where people wept and cried. Maybe the desire for more order has tamped it down. Is our church a place for crying out? We may treasure order too much here. We feel like we have to keep it under control in the church. If you want to cry or weep, it doesn't seem like you can do that in most churches. If you were to start crying or weeping, people might think you're drunk or that you've missed your medication.

In nearby Santa Monica there's a place called the Primal Therapy Center. It is a place where it is okay to cry. In fact, people pay hundreds, maybe even thousands of dollars, to cry and weep there. It is reported that their experts can help bring your repressed pain to conscious awareness so that it can be re-experienced in a therapy session. People spend a lot of money to cry or weep or groan or shout about their pain. I do not belittle them. I only wonder if we, the church, the fellowship of the Great Physician, understand that we have His presence here to help us? That here, in the gathering of our congregation, or any gathering of believers, we have the presence of God, the throne of grace. Hannah wept and cried "before the Lord." Do we know where to go when we are hurting, like Hannah? Psalm 5:2 says,

> Give ear to my words, O Lord, consider my sighing, listen to my cry for help, my King and my God, for to you I pray.

This is the practical theology of Hannah. Like we hear in Psalm.40:1: "He turned to me and heard my cry." Like we hear in Psalm.130:1: "Out of the depths I cry to You, O Lord; O Lord hear my voice!"

Hannah and the psalms show us how meaningful the presence of God is for us when we are hurting and in need.

She Teaches Us to Treasure the Power of God.

She knew the Lord's power, that is, His "sovereignty." To some of us that is an old fashioned word, but it describes God's unlimited rule and power. In 1:11 she refers to God not simply as "Lord" but "Lord of Hosts" or "Lord Almighty" (NIV). Prior to the book of Samuel you cannot find this title given to God. It seems to originate in biblical literature with Hannah. The term "hosts" means all the powers of heaven. God is over all, and everything is subordinate to Him. She understood and believed in that the power. She knew that God could overrule any human frailty, any setback, any disappointment, any hardship. Nothing was too great for Him to overcome and if she knew *Him,* nothing was too great for her to overcome either. Sovereignty means we can rest in Him, whatever the outcome. In verse 17, Eli tells her "to go in peace." She does. So can you. God wants us to rest in Him, to have peace in Him, whatever our prayers may be.

Sometimes there is a disturbance or hold up or trouble in our life, and we become like Los Angeles drivers, ready to lay down on the horn, let it blare, and start yelling, "Hey, God, when is the light going to change! God, things were going great but You switched lanes on me and cut me off! God, everything takes so long, it is miserably slow, when is my life going to get moving?! God, get this idiot out of my way!"

But when you trust God, in a manner of speaking, you give up driving and take the bus. God's sovereignty means this life isn't a car trip. Life under His care is more of a bus ride with all the stops and a little less responsibility. He is driving, taking the route, and the best possible route, for all of us together as His people. When you trust in Him, when you trust in Christ, you essentially surrender your driver's license. You pull up to the cross, get out of your car, kneel down and pray, "Jesus, I believe in You as the Son of God, take my life and let it be consecrated Lord to You." You turn over your car keys to Him. You get on the bus with the rest of us. You give up your right to determine the route, the stops, the speed, and the timing. Do you notice how relaxed people are on the bus? You're sitting in your car, a little tense or worried or miserable and stressed out, focusing on making that left turn before the green turns to yellow (or the yellow turns to red). Maybe you are just inching along in traffic. Then you look at the people alongside of you on the bus. They're chilling out. They're reading. They're listening to music. They're on their phones, connecting with their friends or maybe, eating a sandwich. Christian, I command you, by the power of God, chill out! Read. Listen to music. Connect with your friends. Enjoy a meal. What I mean is that in so far as it depends on you, be at peace with your life and the people around you and with your circumstances. This doesn't mean you cannot take steps to change things in your life, but don't give into frustration with God's providence. If you're on the bus you must trust. And you must trust the route He is taking you.

God answered Hannah's prayer by giving her what she had asked for. She gave Samuel up to the Lord for all the days of his life. But she could only give Samuel up because she had first given herself up to God. We have to know and trust Him, too. Trust on. Pray on. Work on. Fight on. Love on. Weep when you need. Treaure Him, treasure His presence, and His power. He might or might not give us what we pray for, but if He is our God and we are His, the same God who directed Hannah's life is guiding our lives, too.

www.ingramcontent.com/pod-product-compliance
Lightning Source LLC
Chambersburg PA
CBHW052150110526
44591CB00012B/1921